100 steps for science

WHY IT WORKS AND HOW IT HAPPENED

Written by Lisa Jane Gillespie

Illustrated by Yukai Du

WIDE EYED EDITIONS

CONTENTS

SPACE

Long ago, before writing and science were invented, people looked up at the night sky, just as we do today. As they gazed at the stars, they wondered about the universe, and about Earth's place in it.

Just like our ancestors, today we can see thousands of pinpricks of light shining in the night sky, but most are so far away that it takes years for their twinkling light to reach Earth. So, in a way, when we see them we are actually looking back in time.

Stars are glowing balls of burning gas, so they don't actually "twinkle." The light from stars wobbles as it passes through the Earth's atmosphere, making it *seem* like the stars are twinkling.

① MAPPING THE NIGHT SKY

As early as 4000 BC, the ancient Egyptians were charting the stars they could see at night. They realized that as time passed, the stars' positions in the sky changed.

Some historians believe that the Egyptians built their pyramids to align with certain stars. It remains a controversial theory, but many believe that the three pyramids at Giza act like a three-dimensional map of the stars that make up Orion's Belt in the Orion constellation.

② MARKING TIME

By observing the movement of the stars, the Egyptians could keep track of the seasons, hold yearly festivals, and know when to expect the flooding of the River Nile, too.

Between 3000 BC and 2000 BC, Neolithic people in England worked out that stars—including our sun—move in the sky according to the seasons. They built structures like Stonehenge, which had various functions, such as tracking the movement of the stars and helping them to predict the seasons. On the first day of summer (called the summer solstice), you can sit in the center of Stonehenge and see the sun rising exactly over the Heel Stone, shining sunlight directly onto the Altar Stone.

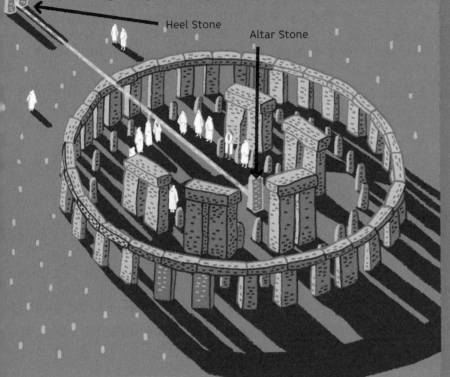

Heel Stone

Altar Stone

Later, about 200 BC, ancient Greek scholars invented clever astronomical devices. By turning the handles of an invention we now call the ANTIKYTHERA MECHANISM to a certain date, they could calculate the positions of stars, determine when eclipses would happen, and predict when the moon would be full.

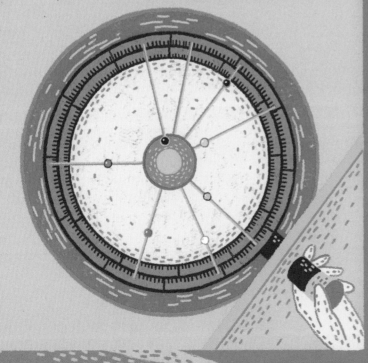

③ NAVIGATING BY THE STARS

Using their understanding of **ASTROLOGY**, the ancient Greeks created an instrument called an **ASTROLABE**. With this instrument, astronomers and mathematicians could chart the movement of the stars very accurately.

Muslim scientists in 8th and 9th century Persia used this information to create their own elaborate astrolabes. From Persia, this science spread to Europe. The mariner's astrolabe came to be used on ships in the 15th century, when sailors navigated by looking at the stars. The technology evolved over time and, in the 18th century, the portable—and more accurate—**SEXTANT** was invented.

To use a sextant, the navigator would look directly at the horizon. Using the moveable arm, he would change the position of the mirror until the light from the sun streamed into the eyepiece.

Then, by checking the position of the arm, he could work out the angle between the horizon and the sun. This allowed him to calculate his LATITUDE—his distance from the equator.

By doing a different calculation, he could also establish his LONGITUDE, and therefore work out his exact position.

④ EARTH'S POSITION IN SPACE

Most ancient civilizations believed that Earth was the center of the universe and that the sun—as well as other planets and stars—revolved around it.

Greek astronomer Aristarchus of Samos didn't agree, though, and proposed in the 3rd century BC that it was the other way around: that Earth orbited the sun.

This idea wouldn't properly catch on for another 1,800 years, when, in 1543, a Polish scientist and astronomer, Nicolaus Copernicus published his book *De revolutionibus orbium coelestium* (*On the Revolutions of the Heavenly Spheres*). In the book, he developed this idea of the Earth's orbit around the sun.

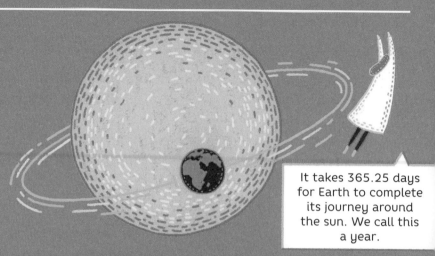

It takes 365.25 days for Earth to complete its journey around the sun. We call this a year.

Sun

Earth

Mercury

Mars

Venus

⑤ THE SOLAR SYSTEM

Copernicus realized that it wasn't only Earth orbiting the sun, and identified six other planets that were also circling it—some closer and others farther away. This set of planets, together with the sun, became known as our **SOLAR SYSTEM**.

Another astronomer, Galileo Galilei, identified the moons of Jupiter and spread the word about Copernicus's sun-centered model of the solar system. The **TELESCOPE** had been invented by the Dutchman Hans Lippershey in 1608, but Galileo was the first to design one to point toward the sky and use it for his astronomical observations.

As telescopes got stronger, new discoveries were made. So far, we know that the solar system is made up of one central star (the sun), eight planets, several dwarf planets (including Pluto), more than 140 moons, millions of asteroids, and billions of comets!

⑥ DAY AND NIGHT

Copernicus's revolutionary book also explained how Earth spins on it axis once every 24 hours, bringing day and night.

The sun is the closest star to Earth. Its light and warmth make life on Earth possible.

1. As the Earth spins, the part facing the sun receives light, making it day. When that part of Earth faces away from the sun, it is blocked from its light, making it night.

2. As the Earth continues to spin, the sun's rays begin to reach that part of Earth again, so the sun looks to us like it is rising in the sky. Later, as night approaches, the sun looks like it is "setting."

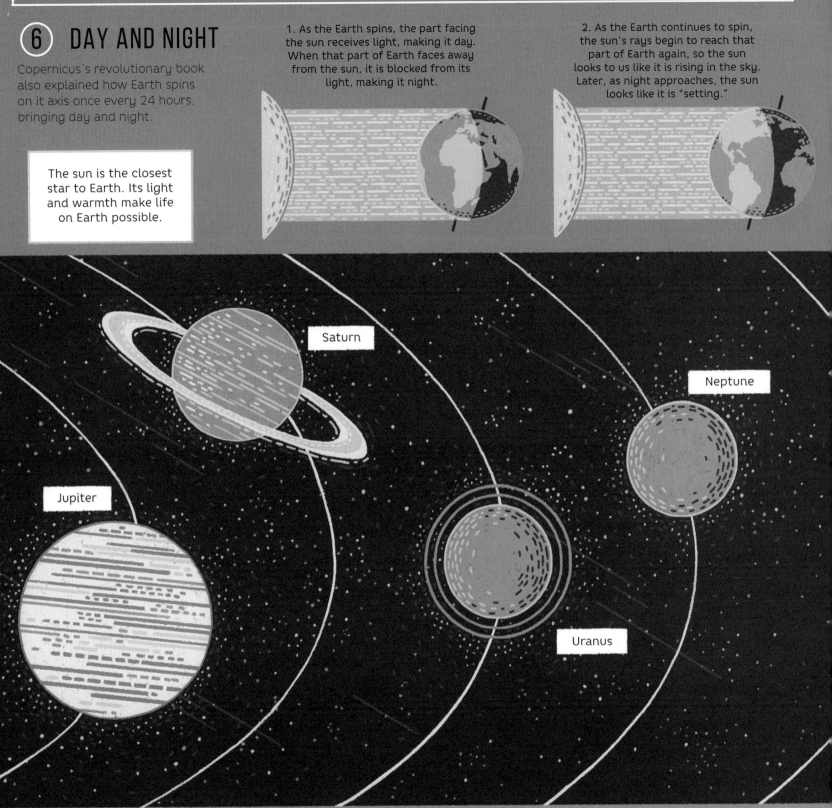

Jupiter

Saturn

Neptune

Uranus

⑦ THE SEASONS

Copernicus's book didn't stop there! In it, he showed that the Earth's orbit around the sun also causes the seasons.

Later, a German astronomer called Johannes Kepler worked out the mathematics behind Copernicus's theories. He developed the idea that the planets orbit the sun in ovals (called ellipses), not circles.

1. The sun spins on a tilted axis. This means that at certain points during the Earth's orbit of the sun, one half of the planet receives more sunlight than the other. For example, when the top half (called the Northern Hemisphere) is tilted toward the sun, it receives more sunlight than the bottom half (the Southern Hemisphere). The part receiving more sunlight experiences summer, while the other part experiences winter.

2. During the course of one complete orbit, Earth's two hemispheres go through a cycle of the four seasons—spring, summer, autumn, and winter. Because they lie at opposite ends of the globe, the Northern and Southern Hemispheres experience the seasons at opposite times of the year.

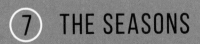

⑧ GRAVITY AND TIDES

Kepler had discovered that the movement of the tides is linked to the moon's orbit of the sun.

Around the year 1700, the scientist Sir Isaac Newton came up with his theory of the **LAW OF UNIVERSAL GRAVITATION**. He combined the theories of Copernicus with the math of Kepler and the astronomical observations of Galileo, along with his own idea of universal gravitation, to describe how the planets and the moon move.

Newton proposed that every object in the universe attracts every other object with a force proportional to its **MASS**.

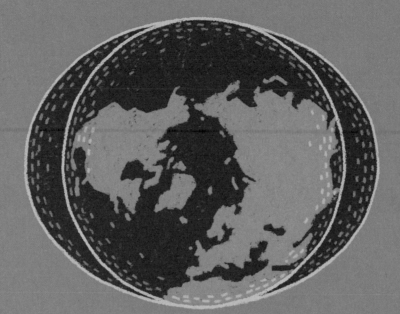

1. The moon orbits the Earth because it is attracted by the Earth's gravity.

2. However, the moon also exerts its gravity on the Earth—the water in the Earth's oceans is attracted to the moon and is pulled toward it.

3. This causes the tides.

⑨ THE BIG BANG

In the 20th century, scientists such as Albert Einstein and Stephen Hawking used mathematics and physics to build up an understanding of how old the universe is. They also worked out how it might have been born, as well as when and how it might die. Today, we think that the universe is 13.8 billion years old.

In 1924, scientists such as the American Edwin Hubble discovered galaxies beyond our own and found that they were moving away from each other. They later learned that the universe used to be smaller and hotter: it has been growing and cooling down for billions of years. The term **BIG BANG** was invented to explain the moment when a tiny speck first exploded incredibly quickly to create the universe.

Since then, the universe has kept growing. There are different theories about whether this will continue to happen or not.

Scientists therorize that the universe could stop growing and stabilize, could contract (The Big Crunch), or could continue until it tears itself apart (The Big Rip).

From that initial tiny speck, the universe continues to expand today.

10 SPACE EXPLORATION

For centuries, humans dreamed of exploring the universe but it only became a reality in 1961, when Yuri Gagarin became the first man in space. His spacecraft made one orbit of the Earth, but he was only in space for one hour and 45 minutes.

In 1969, Americans Neil Armstrong and Buzz Aldrin became the first people to walk on the moon.

Since then, humans have sent unmanned missions to other planets in our solar system, and farther out into the MILKY WAY galaxy.

Our solar system is only a small part of our galaxy, which we call the Milky Way. The Milky Way is made up of billions of stars and our solar system sits on one of its outer arms.

WHEELS

Wheels are an ancient form of technology that we still use today. They exist in obvious places, like cars, and also in places you might not expect, like engines and turbines.

Although humans had been hunting and building things with heavy materials for years, the animals they hunted and the materials they needed were difficult to move. Then came the discovery of wheels, which allowed them to move things more easily...

1 LOG ROLLERS

The first step in the invention of the wheel began during the **PALEOLITHIC ERA** (between 15,000 and 750,000 years ago), with the use of **LOG ROLLERS**. Circular tree stumps carried heavy objects as they turned over the ground. As the heavy object moved forward, the back logs were brought to the front.

Our log rollers paved the way for the invention of the wheel.

FRICTION is a force that makes heavy objects difficult to move. Although friction wasn't properly understood until many hundreds of years later, early humans noticed its effect on heavy objects and looked for ways to overcome it.

Friction makes an object more difficult to move and slows it down. A much greater **PUSHING FORCE** is needed to give the object a **FORWARD MOTION**.

Wheels help to reduce this friction by reducing the amount of contact area between two surfaces. This then reduces the resistant friction that the two surfaces create when they touch one another.

Pushing force

Forward motion

Pushing force

Forward motion

The more **FRICTION** there is, the larger the **PUSHING FORCE** needs to be.

WHEELS reduce friction, meaning less pushing force is needed.

Resistant pull force (friction)

Resistant pull force (friction)

2 THE WHEEL AND AXLE

Today, we are most used to seeing wheels and axles on cars or bikes, but they were first invented for the **POTTER'S WHEEL** in 3500 BC.

At this time, skilled potters in Mesopotamia (now Iraq) quickly spun flat wooden disks by hand, which helped them mold their pottery.

These potters' wheels allowed them to set up factories and produce lots of pots each day.

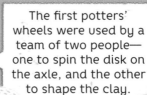

The first potters' wheels were used by a team of two people—one to spin the disk on the axle, and the other to shape the clay.

③ WATER WHEELS

WATER WHEELS date back to the time of the ancient Greeks and Romans. They were also used in China as early as the 1st century. They lifted water in wooden buckets from a river to a dry field, to water crops.

As the wheel spins, water pours out

WATER MILLS worked in a similar way: flowing water turned a wheel that was connected to a stone, which would grind grain into flour.

2. The wheel is connected to a shaft, which it turns.

3. This shaft turns a series of connected cogs.

4. The cogs power the stones that grind the grain.

5. Finally, the grain is poured into bags.

1. Water powers the wheel, causing it to turn.

The wheel captures the moving energy of the water and powers the machinery inside the mill.

The same technology became really useful when a pair of wheels were mounted onto an **AXLE**—a rod connecting the wheels together.

This meant that an object or a person could be carried on a stationary platform, like a chariot, while the wheels rolled freely underneath.

Axle

Wheel

SPOKED WHEELS made our chariots the fastest in the land.

Around 2000 BC, the first chariots with spoked wheels were invented in western Asia. The Persians (modern-day Iran) added to the invention with scythes—long blades—attached to the wheels, giving the Persian army an advantage over their enemies in war.

4 ANCIENT TECHNOLOGY

The invention of wheels later gave rise to other technology. One of the most useful inventions that ancient civilizations created from wheels was the pulley.

In 260 BC the ancient Greek scientist Archimedes invented a really efficient **PULLEY SYSTEM** to help sailors load extremely heavy cargo on and off their ships. A rope moved around a set of wheels to magnify the sailors' strength.

Roman engineers built impressive roads, aqueducts, temples, and amphitheaters throughout their empire. Huge **MULTIPLE-PULLEY CRANES** were operated by people walking around treadmills. They pulled ropes and turned wheels, lifting and moving gigantic stone loads.

How a pulley works:

1. A simple pulley is made from a rope that is wound over a wheel.

By pulling on one side of the rope, a force is transferred to an object connected to the other end of the rope.

> With a straight pulley, 100 lbs of force lifts 100 lbs of mass.

2. Pulleys transfer the direction of the force, so by pulling down on the rope, an object could be lifted upward.

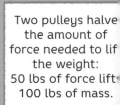

> Two pulleys halve the amount of force needed to lift the weight: 50 lbs of force lifts 100 lbs of mass.

3. By adding more wheels, pulleys can multiply a force to make lifting something easier.

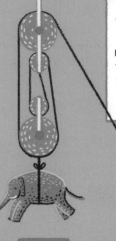

> With four pulleys, the 100 lbs only needs a quarter of the force to lift it: 25 lbs of force lifts 100 lbs of mass.

5 FORCES

As mankind developed machines to help them travel faster, build higher, and lift heavier things, they started to understand more about the **FORCES** acting on an object.

In the 11th century, Persian (modern-day Iran) scholars had experimented to see what forces did to stationary objects: how a push could make an object move, how strong a push was needed for the object to move quickly, and how to stop a moving object.

Later, in 1687, Newton wrote a book called *Principia*. In it he explained his **LAWS OF MOTION**, describing how pushes and pulls make things move, and how the speeds they reach depend on how heavy they are. Take a look at Newton's three laws

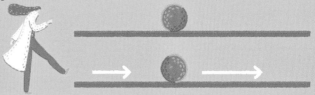

1. An object's motion (whether it is moving, or still) does not change unless a force acts on it. So unless you kick a ball, it will not move.

2. An object's **ACCELERATION** or **DECELERATION** (how much it speeds up or slows down) is affected by its mass and the amount of force exerted on it.

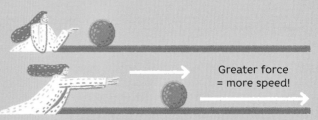

Greater force = more speed!

3. All forces act in pairs, so for every force applied to an object, an equal and opposite force is created. This explains why a ball bounces back up when you throw it down to the floor, or bounces away from you when you throw it at an angle.

6 SIMPLE MACHINES

Wheels and pulleys were just two of six **SIMPLE MACHINES** to be known and used by early inventors. A simple machine is a device that helps change the direction or increase strength of a force. They all allow a person to move an object more easily, by multiplying a force.

Leonardo da Vinci was a talented scientist, inventor, and artist of the 15th century, who made sketches and models of many machines, including complicated pulley systems. Some of his ideas were so advanced that the materials to build them wouldn't exist until the 20th century.

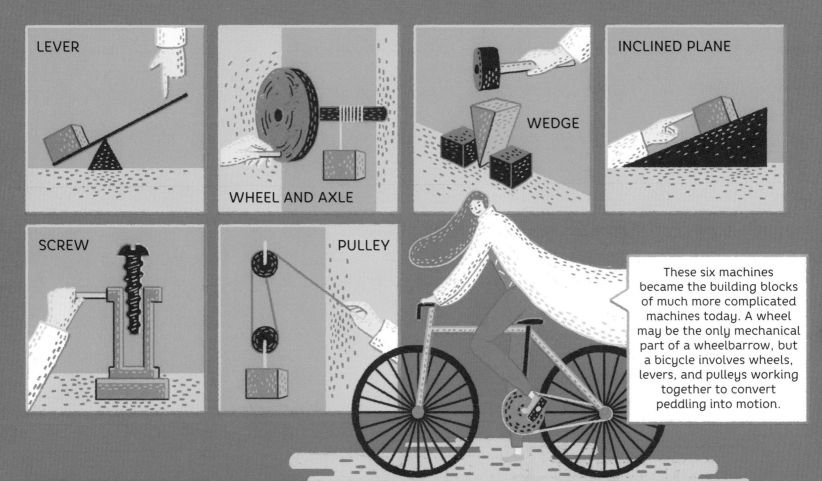

LEVER

WHEEL AND AXLE

WEDGE

INCLINED PLANE

SCREW

PULLEY

These six machines became the building blocks of much more complicated machines today. A wheel may be the only mechanical part of a wheelbarrow, but a bicycle involves wheels, levers, and pulleys working together to convert peddling into motion.

7 GEARS

During the 18th and 19th centuries, many ingenious inventors in Europe and North America created intricate machines. The machines all involved moving parts, including wheels, pulleys, cogs, and **GEARS**. These machines meant that products could be manufactured easily. Many factories were founded to make clothes, books, food, and metal at a faster pace—and by fewer people—than ever before.
  Many people moved from the countryside to take up new jobs working with these machines. They lived in cramped cities and worked in dangerous factories for low wages. This period of rapid change became known as the **INDUSTRIAL REVOLUTION**.

A small force can turn a small gear wheel, which turns a larger wheel. This makes the force stronger, so the larger wheel can move something heavier than the smaller wheel could move alone.

GEARS are sets of turning, interlocking wheels that have teeth around their rims. One wheel's teeth touches the teeth of other wheels, so when the first wheel (the driver gear) is turned by a handle, they all turn.

Bigger and faster machines were invented during the Industrial Revolution, which could power whole factories. At this time, there was a huge increase in the number of factories in Europe, especially textile factories and mills.

8 ENGINES

Another invention associated with the Industrial Revolution is the engine. Most engines transform heat energy into **KINETIC ENERGY**, or motion.
  The Victorians burned coal to create steam from water. As the pressure from the steam built up, it caused pistons to pump back and forth. These pistons were connected to rods, which were attached to wheels. As the wheels turned, they would move an object, like a train.
  English engineer Robert Stephenson designed the *Rocket*, the first successful passenger **STEAM LOCOMOTIVE**. It had a pair of large front wheels connected to the engine, which pulled the carriages along. All the wheels were wooden, with spokes, and had metal rims.

9 TURBINES

A **TURBINE** is a kind of wheel that has been adapted to capture the moving energy of a liquid or a gas, and transform it into mechanical energy, which can power a machine. Windmills work in this way, using the moving energy of wind to rotate heavy stones and grind grain into flour.

This machinery evolved to be used in jet engines, which power planes, and to generate electricity in power stations. It has also inspired the technology used to build the shuttles that took humans into outer space.

1. In a jet engine, cold air is sucked into the engine by a fan. The air is compressed and kerosene is squirted in, causing it to burn and give off hot gas fumes.

2. The hot gas cause the blades of the turbine to spin, which powers the fan at the front.

3. The hot gas is then funneled out of the back of the engine through a thin exhaust nozzle. As it gets compressed into the thin nozzle—a smaller space—the gas moves quicker under pressure.

4. The fast speed of the gas leaving the engine powers the plane, causing it to move forward.

10 RENEWABLE ENERGY

Just like the water wheels and windmills dating back thousands of years, today we use giant wheels called **WIND TURBINES**.

Modern wind turbines capture the energy of moving air, thanks to their huge blades, which are turned by the wind. Wind is a kind of **RENEWABLE ENERGY** because it is naturally produced and cannot run out, and has a low impact on the environment.

1. A wind turbine's blades capture the kinetic energy of the wind. They spin, which rotates a shaft inside the turbine.

Gearbox

2. The rotating shaft is connected to a gearbox, which increases the rotation speed.

The gearbox is connected to a generator, which converts the kinetic energy of the wind into the electrical energy that lights our homes.

Gas-powered **CARS** were first developed in the1880s. By 1908, they were being made on an industrial scale in large factories. They had rubber tires around their metal wheels, and wheels, cogs, and gears were important parts of their engines and steering mechanisms.

NUMBERS

It seems strange to think that there was once a time before humans had invented numbers, but this was one of our most important discoveries: without numbers, it is impossible to count and measure things, or to write down and record amounts.

Once we had figured out how to count with numbers, humans were able to record the passing of time. This meant they were able to predict the changing seasons and become better farmers.

1 COUNTING

Humans probably always needed to count, to know how many children were in their tribe or how many cows were in a herd.

Before numbers—or names for numbers—existed, people might have used their fingers, thumbs, and toes. But when they needed to count higher they began to use tallies—these are simple groups of lines or sticks that help keep track of counts of three, five or ten.

As early as 1800 BC, early humans made tally marks on cave walls, on stone, and on pieces of bone.

> The ISHANGO BONE, found in Africa, is the oldest-known counting record at over 20,000 years old. But exactly what its owner counted is a mystery...

2 NUMERALS

In 3000 BC, scribes in ancient Egypt recorded their harvests by using **HIEROGLYPHIC NUMBERS** instead of tallies. These helped them work out the amount of wheat that could be grown in a certain size of field, how much bread to give workers, and how many crops could be stored in a warehouse.

③ MEASURING TIME

Ancient people wanted to measure time periods, and did this by counting the passing time. They made the first CALENDARS on stone pillars, papyrus scrolls, and clay tablets. These were based on the movement of the sun and the moon. They measured days, months, and years. In 500 BC, Central American tribes carved numbers onto stone pillars to measure the seasons and years. The Aztec calendar is one of the most recognizable. It was made up of two separate calendars: One calendar, called xiuhpohualli, had 365 days and focused on the seasons, or an agricultural year. The second, tonalpohualli, had 260 days, and was a sacred calendar, dividing up days of the year to worship different gods.

The ancient Greeks and Romans both used HOURS as a timescale, counting 12 hours of darkness and 12 hours of daylight. However, the length of an hour would change as the days became longer and shorter according to the seasons! Finally, in the 2nd century BC, Hipparchus suggested a system of a standard hour length. These hours were not easy to measure until mechanical clocks were invented in China during the 1st century.

Calendars meant that people could harvest crops at the same time each year, and mark important days with religious ceremonies.

In 1800 BC, the ancient Babylonians had a way of writing numbers down by pressing reeds into clay tablets and leaving them to dry in the sun. They had symbols for numbers and counted in groups of 60.

The Babylonian way of counting survives today in how we divide an hour into 60 minutes and a minute into 60 seconds.

4 ARITHMETIC

As early as 2000 BC in ancient Egypt and Babylon, people started to use numbers to solve problems, and developed ways of adding, subtracting, multiplying, and dividing. These calculations are types of **ARITHMETIC**—one of the earliest branches of mathematics.

COMPUTING means figuring out the answer to a question. Early computers, such as mechanical calculators, helped people do difficult calculations much faster than by hand. The earliest computer—an **ABACUS**—was invented in Sumer (modern-day southern Iraq). By moving the position of the beads, the user could make calculations to keep track of business deals or money. This idea spread quickly and several variations were made across Europe, China, and Russia.

5 ZERO—AND BELOW!

Around 2,000 years ago in ancient China, people used **COUNTING RODS**, which they arranged in different positions to represent numbers.

Using their red counting rods, Chinese mathematicians could do calculations where the final answer was "no rods." Then they realized that if you took a big number away from a small number there could be numbers that were negative. They represented these negative answers using black rods.

Thinking in the same way as the Chinese scholars, an Indian mathematician, Brahmagupta, developed the idea of a "nothing" answer to a calculation. In the 7th century AD, he was the first to write about this "nothingness" being an actual number. He called it **ZERO** and he gave it the symbol "0."

We indicate that a number is negative by inserting a minus sign in front of it.

Today we call the numbers that we normally count with POSITIVE NUMBERS (the "red rod" numbers). We call the numbers that are less than zero NEGATIVE NUMBERS (the "black rod" numbers). Negative numbers are important for measuring temperatures, keeping track of finances, and in the scoring of some games.

⑥ DECIMAL SYSTEM

Between the 1st and 4th centuries in India, mathematicians started working with a system of counting based on groups of 10. This idea spread far and wide, becoming popular because of how easily the symbols could be written and used in calculations.

It became know as **THE DECIMAL SYSTEM** and today it is the most common way that we use numbers around the world. It makes writing large numbers easy because of **PLACE VALUE:** each symbol has a different value of ten depending on its overall position in the number.

WHOLE NUMBERS

DECIMAL FRACTIONS

6 9 0 5 . 0 7 2 8

THOUSANDS
HUNDREDS
TENS
ONES
DECIMAL POINT
TENTHS
HUNDREDTHS
THOUSANDTHS
TEN-THOUSANDTHS

Here is how it works…

⑦ GEOMETRY

Pythagoras was a Greek mathematician living in the 6th century BC. He was interested in odd and even numbers, and in **GEOMETRY**. He believed that numbers ruled the universe and he set up schools where men and women could study science and mathematics.

Euclid was a mathematician who studied the work of Pythagoras and other mathematicians. He combined them with his own ideas about shapes and numbers in his great book, called *Elements*.

Geometry is the mathematics of lines, shapes, areas, and volumes. There are ancient geometry equations that helped people calculate the height of a pyramid, the area of a circular field, and the volume of a cylindrical grain store.

8 ALGEBRA

In the 9th and 10th centuries, another branch of mathematics called
ALGEBRA was developed in the Middle East. Instead of working with
exact numbers, algebra allowed mathematicians to use "mystery"
numbers (often represented by letters such as "x") in calculations.

This was useful for mathematicians and engineers who wanted to
explain the world around us by working out answers to calculations.
Their sums often involved unknown or variable numbers, related to
measures like speed and gravity.

$$E=mc^2$$

Over time, mathematicians worked out ever-more complex
algebraic equations—the most famous of which is probably
Albert Einstein's THEORY OF RELATIVITY. It states that $E=mc^2$,
where an object's kinetic energy (E) is equal to its mass (m)
multiplied by the speed of light squared (c^2).

9 MATHEMATICAL MACHINES

As mathematicians developed more complex calculations, they
began to develop machines to help them. In 1617, John Napier
made a set of carved rods called NAPIER'S BONES to help multiply
and divide large numbers. Then, in 1630, the SLIDE RULE was
created by William Oughtred, to perform multiplication and
division. In 1820, Thomas de Colmar went on to mass-produce
counting machines called ARITHMOMETERS.

Charles Babbage designed the first mechanical computers
with Ada Lovelace. Their ANALYTICAL ENGINE would answer
complicated calculations faster than a human, but it was never
completely finished, due to a lack of funds. It would have been
powered by steam, gears, and rods, which would move in
sequence to generate answers that a printing press would print.
Ada developed a series of codes, which could be made
into patterns of holes punched in tiny cards.

Ada's codes would tell the
machine how to calculate the
correct answers. She was the
first computer programmer.

10 MODERN COMPUTING

Computing machines—COMPUTERS—caught on, and between 1943 and 1946 the US Army developed ENIAC, the first general-use electronic computer.

It was nicknamed "Giant Brain" and was so big that it filled a huge basement at the University of Pennsylvania.

As the technology developed, it got smaller. Pocket CALCULATORS were invented in the late 1960s, when new, tiny electrical components allowed simple calculations to be performed on portable machines. MICROCHIPS, were perfected in the 1970s, which stored lots of information in BINARY CODE and meant that computers could shrink from room-size machines to personal devices.

Electronic computers use electrical signals, microchips, and programs, instead of mechanical parts. By the 1980s, design had advanced so far that computing machines were small and affordable enough to be found in homes—as desktop computers and game consoles.

Computers store information and programs using binary code. Binary numbers are written using only 1s and 0s. In coding, 1 stands for "yes" or "on," and 0 stands for "no" or "off." Binary numbers were first used in China hundreds of year ago—which goes to show how even the most advanced technology has its roots in ancient knowledge!

During the Second World War, the British wanted to break secret codes sent by enemy troops. Mathematician Alan Turing designed an electromechanical computer called THE BOMBE. It used lots of drums to run thousands of calculations to decipher secret messages.

LIGHT

Light comes from shining sources, the sun, a fire, a torch, a screen, or a lightbulb.

There were many theories in the ancient world about whether our eyes absorbed or emitted light. It would take hundreds and hundreds of years before humans would understand light and begin to use instruments to adapt and capture it.

① VISION

Around the 4th century BC, a philosopher known as Plato believed that humans could see because beams of light shined out of our eyes, like torches, highlighting objects in front of us. For hundreds of years, people agreed with his **EMISSION THEORY**.

Much later, in the 11th century, a scholar known in Europe as Alhazen wrote *The Book of Optics*. He discussed how light reflects and bends, and suggested that we see because light is reflected from objects in straight lines and enters our eyes. In the 13th century, Englishman Roger Bacon also proved that light reflects from objects.

② OPTICS

Early on, humans noticed that light behaves differently in different conditions. For instance, when light enters water, objects can appear closer than they actually are.

As early as the 3rd century BC, the mathematician Euclid, who had been working on theories about geometry, studied the behavior of light. Around the same time, the Greeks and Romans created basic versions of **LENSES** by filling glasses with water.

Light travels in perfectly straight lines, but there are three main ways in which we can control its direction.

1. It can be blocked by an object that absorbs its rays.

This creates a shadow.

2. It can be reflected by a mirror.

If light hits a mirror, it bounces off in the opposite direction.

3. It can be refracted as it travels through a transparent object, like water.

REFRACTION is when light changes direction as it passes through something.

Refraction

As the light enters the object, it slows down, which can also create optical illusions.

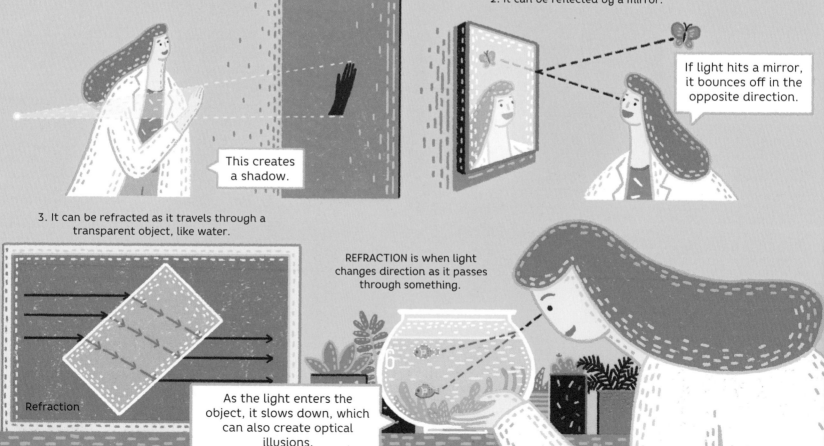

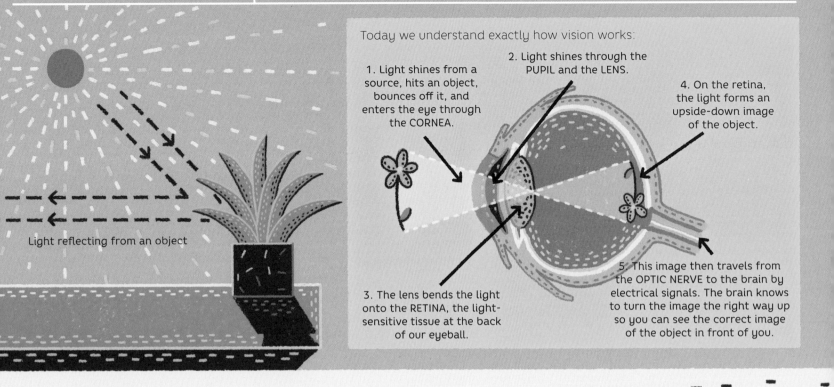

Today we understand exactly how vision works:

1. Light shines from a source, hits an object, bounces off it, and enters the eye through the CORNEA.

2. Light shines through the PUPIL and the LENS.

4. On the retina, the light forms an upside-down image of the object.

3. The lens bends the light onto the RETINA, the light-sensitive tissue at the back of our eyeball.

5. This image then travels from the OPTIC NERVE to the brain by electrical signals. The brain knows to turn the image the right way up so you can see the correct image of the object in front of you.

Light reflecting from an object

③ LENSES

In 13th century England, Roger Bacon began experimenting with refraction and created early magnifying glasses using lenses. At a similar time in Italy, pioneering glassmakers created early designs of spectacles. Two magnifying lenses were placed in a frame and made objects seem bigger—and clearer—to shortsighted people. The idea may have come to Europe with traders returning from China and India.

Magnifying lens

In the 1590s in the Netherlands, glassmakers Hans and Zacharias Janssen made the first **MICROSCOPES**, which helped make tiny objects appear larger. A series of lenses helped to make images nine times larger. In the 17th century, the scientist Antonie van Leeuwenhoek was able to develop lenses that were much more powerful.

The opposite effect can be created with a **CONCAVE LENS**, which makes objects appear smaller.

If you've ever looked through a peephole in a door, you will have seen how they work.

4 SEEING DISTANT OBJECTS

In 17th century Italy, Galileo created a type of telescope that allowed him to see the night sky more clearly. His arrangement of lenses magnified objects by 30 times, so he could observe the moons of Jupiter—more than 365 million miles away.

Later, in the 18th century, a new lens—called an ACHROMATIC LENS—was invented. This reduced the distortion of the earlier models and made it even easier to see the night sky.

There are lots of different kinds of telescopes that exist today, but one of the simplest is the REFLECTOR TELESCOPE. It uses small curved mirrors that reflect the light and concentrate it, allowing us to see objects that are farther away. Sir Isaac Newton created one of the first telescopes of this kind in 1688.

Reflector telescope

6 ELECTROMAGNETIC SPECTRUM

White light (and the colors it's made of) are only part of a family of types of wave energies called the ELECTROMAGNETIC SPECTRUM. Some types of energy on the spectrum are bigger waves than light, and others are smaller. They are invisible to the naked eye but they surround us every day. We use them for communication, cooking, and medical treatments.

William Herschel was the first scientist to discover an electromagnetic wave other than light in 1800. He found that high temperatures could be detected just beyond the color red—which came to be known as INFRARED. The next year, Johann Ritter detected ULTRAVIOLET RADIATION at the other end of the scale, beyond violet.

| Radio waves | Microwaves | Infrared | Visible | Ultraviolet |

5 SPLITTING WHITE LIGHT

The sun's light appears to us as a white light, but it is actually made up of different colors—red, orange, yellow, green, blue, indigo, and violet. It can be split into these colors by refraction, when light bends as it changes direction. You can see this when light shines through a mist of raindrops and forms a rainbow, or sometimes when it shines through a glass of water.

In 1307, the physicist Theodoric of Freiberg carried out experiments showing that rainbows are formed by raindrops, which refract—or change the direction of—sunlight as it passes through them.

Later, in 1666, Newton used a piece of quartz glass—a **PRISM**—to split white light into its component colors. He gave names to each of the seven colors, which together form the **COLOR SPECTRUM**.

White light

Prism

In 1960, T.H. Maiman developed the first working LASER, a beam of concentrated light energy. Since then, lasers have been used as scanners, in DVD machines, in laser surgery, and for cutting and welding metal.

There were many other discoveries to follow, too. In 1886 Heinrich Hertz detected **RADIO WAVES** and **MICROWAVES**. Then, in 1895, Wilhelm Röntgen discovered **X-RAYS**, and in 1900 Paul Villard discovered **GAMMA RAYS**.

Radio waves are invisible to us but they are wider than a football field!

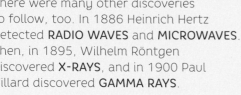

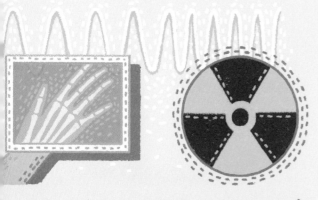

X-rays   Gamma rays

7 THE SPEED OF LIGHT

As scientists began to understand that light came from the sun to the Earth, they started to think about how fast it could travel.

The astronomer Ole Rømer went to Paris in 1676 and recorded the eclipses of Jupiter's moons. He then did a series of calculations to estimate the speed of light as 131,000 miles per second. This was lower than the true speed we know today, which is 186,000 miles per second, but he wasn't far off!

Knowing the speed of light is helpful when measuring enormous distances in space. Astronomers use **LIGHT-YEARS** as a measurement, which describes the distance that light travels in that time. For instance, the Andromeda galaxy is about 2.5 million light-years away from Earth...

...which is easier to say than 14,696,563,000,000,000,000 miles!

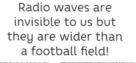

8 WAVES, PARTICLES, AND PHOTONS

But what is light actually made of? Back in the 1660s, Newton thought of light as a beam made of **PARTICLES**—solid objects, with definite shapes, like a tiny balls, which could act independently of each other.

Scientists Robert Hooke and Christiaan Huygens were studying light at the same time as Newton. They believed in a **WAVE** theory, which was based on the idea that light was made of waves. Just like those at sea, waves could spread out in all directions and move together, carrying energy from one place to another.

Later, in 1905, Albert Einstein wondered if light could have properties of both particles and waves, so he developed **PHOTON** theory. Photons are tiny little packets of energy and behave in a way that is sometimes particle-like and sometimes wave-like. Scientists now believe that light is made up of these photons.

This discovery of photons led scientists to develop a whole new branch of thinking, called QUANTUM PHYSICS.

9 CAPTURING LIGHT

CAMERAS capture light and allow us to make images of the world around us—to freeze a moment and see it forever. The first cameras were machines used by artists to shine an image onto a piece of paper, which they could then trace around. The light didn't create a picture, though.

Louis Daguerre (1787–1851) invented commercial photography. He used copper plates, silver, and the chemical mercury to burn images onto the metal using light. Later, pictures were printed on photographic film, first in black and white and then in color. Today, digital cameras are more commonly used. These turn light into electrical signals that create an image on-screen.

Photography enthusiasts discovered that by projecting still images quickly, one after the other, you could create the illusion of **MOVING PICTURES**. One of the first ever movies to be shown to the public was *Arrival of the Train* by the Lumière brothers in 1896. It was only 50 seconds long but looked so realistic that the audience was amazed as the train came closer on the screen.

Around 30 years later, two types of **TELEVISION** were invented—mechanical and electronic. A competition was held and the electronic system came out top because the image was clearer. The first regular television broadcasts were made by the BBC in 1936.

Today, our television broadcasts are in color, our cameras are digital, and our movies can be 3-D. Computer games and films often use motion-capture cameras to record how actors move. Animated features are then projected onto their movements to create fictional, moving characters.

10 FIBER-OPTIC COMMUNICATIONS

FIBER-OPTIC CABLES carry a wealth of information every minute across televisions, phones, and the Internet. The cables are made up of bundles of fiber-optic strands—each strand is a long piece of glass that is the width of a human hair.

Transmitters turn binary information into pulses of light. The light travels through the cables by **REFLECTION**—it bounces efficiently along the length of the cable. At the other end, a receiver turns the light pulses back into binary information so that you can stream a movie or listen to music.

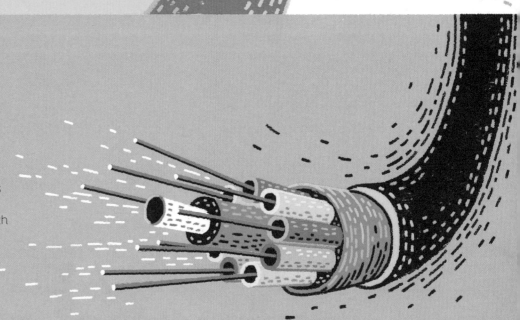

SOUND

Humans have always used sound to communicate: before there was language, humans used grunts and gasps. Then we learned how to laugh, to speak, to sing, to whistle, to use drums, and to make music.

It took humans centuries to overcome the challenges of capturing sound, transmitting it across long distances, and re-creating it with loudspeakers. But once we did, we changed the way we communicate with each other—and entertain ourselves—forever.

① SOUND WAVES

As far back as the 4th century BC, the Greek philosopher Aristotle wondered about how sound reached his ear. He thought that the sound of a bell might travel in waves through the air.

Today we know that sound is a type of energy, and that it is created by a vibrating object. Its **VIBRATIONS** disturb the air around it and cause more vibrations, which spread out in all directions. These vibrations cause even more and more vibrations, moving away from the object, so the sound travels through the air in waves. When the vibrations reach our ears, they make our eardrums vibrate, too—and we hear the sound.

Sound waves need a **MEDIUM** (a solid, liquid, or gas, such as air) to move through. So if you were out in space, you wouldn't be able to hear yourself speaking. We know this because, in 1660, Englishman Robert Boyle conducted an experiment to see if sound needs air to travel. He placed a ticking watch in a flask and removed all the air, and found that the ticking sound couldn't be heard!

How our ears work:

Sound waves enter the ear.

1. The sound waves make the EARDRUM vibrate.

2. The eardrum makes the EAR BONES vibrate.

3. This makes the fluid in the INNER EAR vibrate.

4. The AUDITORY NERVE takes the message to the brain.

② ACOUSTICS

The ancient Greeks and Romans studied how sound behaves in large spaces. They designed their theaters to amplify the voices of the actors so everyone in the audience—even people at the back—would hear them clearly. Some of these ancient amphitheaters still exist today, and you can hear the actors as clearly in the back row as right at the front.

Scientists still study sound waves in this way today, calling this branch of science ACOUSTICS.

3 SPEED OF SOUND

Just like light, sound waves can reflect. These reflections are called ECHOES.

In 1640, in France, Marin Mersenne observed how long his voice took to bounce back as an echo. By doing this, he estimated the speed of sound close to today's measurement of 761 miles per hour.

4 MEASURING SOUND

During the 17th century, Galileo was interested in PITCH— how high or low a sound is. By scraping a chisel across a brass plate, he worked out that FREQUENCY (the number of sound waves per second) controls a sound's pitch. We measure frequency in a unit called HERTZ. Humans can hear sounds between 20 hertz and 20 kilohertz (20,000).

The size of a sound's vibrations (or AMPLITUDE) controls how noisy it is…the bigger the amplitude, the louder the sound. We measure a sound's loudness in DECIBELS. Humans can hear sounds between 0 and 140 decibels, and sounds above 85 decibels can damage your hearing.

⑤ TELECOMMUNICATIONS

Inventors of the 19th century wanted to use their understanding of sound to find ways to transmit it over long distances. The inventor Alexander Graham Bell created one of the earliest versions of the **TELEPHONE**, but even once he had perfected his invention and it was available to the public to buy, it took decades for most households to have one. They were large, clunky pieces of furniture at first and the sound was not very clear.

> When a person talks, the sound of their voice travels in waves into the receiver. This makes a small disk vibrate, causing an electrical signal to be transmitted to the other end of the line. There, a speaker turns the current back into sound.

⑥ RECORDING SOUND

For thousands of years, every word that was spoken and every song that was sung was lost. There was no way of recording it and hearing it again later on. Then the American inventor Thomas Edison developed the **CYLINDER PHONOGRAPH** in 1877. Sound was recorded onto wax cylinders by converting vibrations into grooves. When a needle ran along these grooves, the vibrations were re-created and sound was heard.

Around ten years later, another inventor, Emile Berliner, invented the **DISC PHONOGRAPH**, which used a flat disc, called a **RECORD**, instead of a cylinder.

Large horns amplified the sound, which was very clear. Before long, most households played music on a phonograph.

CASSETTE recording machines had been used by governments and police for decades but by the 1960s they were small and cheap enough for the public to buy. Then came the invention of the **CD**—or compact disc—in the 1980s.

Music became portable for the first time when Walkmans and boom boxes came on the market. Suddenly, you could use a moveable music device to make your music mobile—whether on a CD or cassette.

> Music is now digital. We play it on tiny digital devices that fit in the palms of our hands.

⑦ RADIO

In the 1890s, lots of scientists were investigating an invisible type of electromagnetic energy wave: **RADIO**. They tried different ways of transmitting and receiving the waves, which would eventually become a wireless way of communicating.

In 1899, Italian scientist Guglielmo Marconi sent a coded message of sounds in dots and dashes from France to England, along these invisible air waves. The message was received loud and clear. Soon, ships were using this system—**MORSE CODE**—to send distress signals when they ran into trouble at sea. By the 1920s, these waves were being used to send the human voice out into the air: words, songs, and music were transmitted. The radio, and mass communication, was born.

8 BREAKING THE SOUND BARRIER

The speed of sound is 761 miles per hour. This is the **SOUND BARRIER**: anything that travels faster than this will break through the barrier.

For many years, engineers and pilots wanted to go faster than the speed of sound. It was first achieved by Chuck Yeager in 1947, flying a Bell X-1 aircraft. Most planes don't reach these speeds but some fighter jets do.

Even the Concorde passenger plane could travel at twice the speed of sound. Concorde flights started in 1976 and flew from Paris or London to New York in less than half the time of a normal plane. It stopped service in 2003 because the system was too expensive to maintain.

When a plane breaks the sound barrier, it creates a sound called a **SONIC BOOM,** which can be heard by people on the ground. This is a really loud noise, like an explosion, and it is caused by the number of sound waves being forced together by the fast-moving plane.

9 ECHOLOCATION

Sounds can also help us see. Bats and dolphins use **ECHOLOCATION**. They send out sounds and wait for the echo to return so that they know how close an object is and where they are in relation to it.

In 1906, the scientist Lewis Nixon used a similar idea to invent a machine that detected icebergs. This technology developed into **SONAR**, which is used by research ships and navy ships. They send out pulses of high-energy sound and use the echoes reflected back to find out what's around the ship. This scanning technique creates images of the seafloor, pods of whales, or enemy ships.

10 ULTRASOUND IMAGING

In a similar way to sonar, **ULTRASOUND IMAGING** bounces high-energy sound waves at body tissues, and detects the echoes that bounce back.

The Scottish physician Ian Donald pioneered the use of ultrasound waves in the 1950s. Since the 1970s, doctors and vets have been using it to see the insides of their patients. They can even check on a baby as it grows inside its mother.

PARTICLES

Some areas of science, like astronomy, involve enormous objects on a planetary scale, vast distances that we may never travel, and unimaginably huge numbers. But on the opposite end of the spectrum, in the world right under our noses, are the minuscule building blocks of life. Everything around us is made up of incredibly small particles that we cannot even see with the naked eye.

① ATOMS

ATOMS are tiny, minuscule building blocks that make up everything in the universe—from the biggest planet to the hairs on your head. They are such tiny particles that they can only be seen through a special kind of microscope.

As far back as the 6th century BC, science scholars in India suspected that everything was made of little building blocks. But it wasn't until the 5th century BC, in Greece, that the philosopher Democritus gave these blocks a name: "atomos." He chose this word because it means "indivisible" and he believed that atoms could not be divided into anything smaller.

② ELEMENTS

Any solid, liquid, or gas is made up of millions and millions of tiny atoms joined together by invisible pulling forces. Atoms come in different sizes. Over a hundred different types have been discovered. These different types are known as **ELEMENTS**. The word "element" was first used by the Greek philosopher Plato in 360 BC, but he mistakenly thought that elements were made of earth, air, water, and fire.

It wasn't until nearly 2,000 years later that scientists began to uncover some of the elements we recognize today. In 1789, the French nobleman Antoine Lavoisier wrote *Elementary Treatise on Chemistry*, where he compiled a list elements for the first time. Although some of the things he included in his

list were wrong, he also predicted the existence of others, like silicon, before they had even been discovered. He is called the "Father of Modern Chemistry."

Working on Democritus's theory, in 1803 Englishman John Dalton figured out that all atoms of a particular element are identical, and that they are different than the atoms of another element.

Oxygen, gold, hydrogen, and carbon are examples of elements. They each have their own appearance and properties and are given chemical symbols. For instance, oxygen's symbol is O and hydrogen's symbol is H. Today, there are 118 known elements, and scientists are still adding to the list.

③ MOLECULES, COMPOUNDS, AND MIXTURES

In 1803, the scientist John Dalton proposed a modern theory about atoms.

When atoms are linked to each other through a chemical bond, they form bigger particles called **MOLECULES**. When those atoms come from different elements instead of one single element, they form a **COMPOUND**.

Water is a compound—it's made of molecules that each contain two atoms of hydrogen and one atom of oxygen.

The compound is written H_2O, because it marries together two hydrogen atoms and one oxygen atom. Compounds can only be separated through a chemical reaction.

If you blend compounds together *without* a chemical reaction—like pouring salt into water—you simply have a **MIXTURE**. You can separate mixtures using techniques like **FILTRATION**, **CHROMATOGRAPHY**, **EVAPORATION**, and **DISTILLATION**.

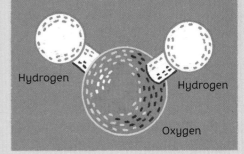

Water is a compound—it has atoms that come from two different elements, hydrogen and oxygen.

Hydrogen

Hydrogen

Oxygen

Distillation can be used to separate a mixture of water and salty water. The water evaporates when it is heated, leaving behind the salt.

④ THE PERIODIC TABLE

Many different elements were discovered during the 18th and 19th centuries. Chemists studied them and knew that some elements behaved in similar ways, whereas others were very different from each other. Some were metals; others weren't. Some were solid; others were liquids and others were gases.

By the 1860s scientists began trying to list the known elements in a logical way based on their behaviors. In 1871, a Russian chemist, Dmitri Mendeleev, tried arranging them on a table, in order of how heavy their atoms were. He noticed that there were repeating patterns. He made his table reflect those patterns by arranging the elements into vertical groups. He even left gaps for elements that he predicted should exist but had not yet been discovered.

This **PERIODIC TABLE** was such a clever and useful way of looking at the elements, and presenting information about them, that scientists still use it today.

⑤ SUBATOMIC PARTICLES

Once scientists began thinking about atoms, they then began to wonder if there might be anything inside an atom; are they solid or are they made of even smaller parts? They tried to work out what those smaller parts might be and if there was any way to break an atom apart. But those experiments wouldn't be possible until the 20th century.

Although scientists such as John Dalton initially suggested, like Democritus, that atoms were indivisible, we now know that they are made of tinier particles. These are **SUBATOMIC PARTICLES** called **PROTONS**, **NEUTRONS**, and **ELECTRONS**.

Protons are found in the **NUCLEUS**—the dense center of an atom. Each proton has a positive electric charge. In 1911, New Zealand physicist Ernest Rutherford and his colleagues used experiments to prove that the nucleus exists and that it's the home of protons.

Neutrons are also found in the nucleus. They are the same size as protons but they have no electric charge—they are neutral. In 1932, the Englishman James Chadwick designed an experiment to locate neutrons in the nucleus of an atom.

In 1897, the English scientist J.J. Thomson and his research team conducted experiments to prove the existence of electrons. Electrons are found outside the nucleus and have a negative electric charge. They are much smaller than protons and neutrons.

6 ATOMIC MODELS

As they learn more and have more experimental evidence, scientists keep adapting how they imagine atoms. These ideas are known as **ATOMIC MODELS**.

The physicist Ernest Rutherford believed that there was a core to each atom, the nucleus, and that most of an atom's weight—the protons and neutrons—were located there. In 1913, Niels Bohr expanded Rutherford's ideas to come up with the Rutherford-Bohr model. He suggested that electrons were found in rings, or shells, around the nucleus. The electrons moved around in these shells, orbiting the nucleus at high speeds, never staying still.

Today scientists use evidence from complicated experiments and mathematical equations to think about atoms and use computers to generate images of electron shells.

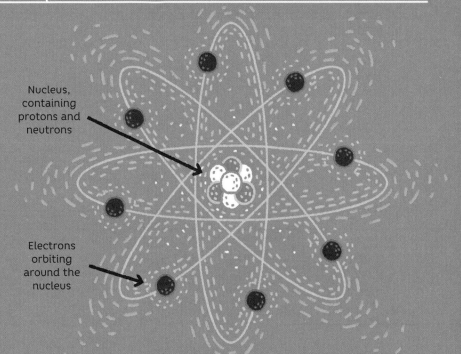

Nucleus, containing protons and neutrons

Electrons orbiting around the nucleus

7 RADIOACTIVITY

Some types of atoms are unstable. They are called **RADIOACTIVE** atoms. They have so many neutrons and are so heavy that they can't remain intact for long. They begin to break down to form a different type of atom. In the process, tiny particles and electromagnetic energy is released. This release is called **RADIATION** and can be harmful.

Henri Becquerel was the first to discover radioactive decay in 1896 in France. Husband-and-wife team Pierre and Marie Curie studied radioactive elements and discovered more, including polonium and radium. Their pioneering work led to the dawn of the **NUCLEAR AGE**.

8 NUCLEAR FISSION

A reaction that causes the radioactive decay of atoms is called **NUCLEAR FISSION**. These reactions are dangerous and powerful.

Scientists first studied fission in the middle of the 20th century. This era became known as the nuclear age, when countries began to use nuclear power and to arm themselves with atomic bombs.

J.R. Oppenheimer lead the US team that created the first atomic bombs, which were dropped on the Japanese cities of Hiroshima and Nagasaki in 1945. The cities were destroyed and thousands of people died in the explosion. Even more got sick from the radiation.

However, nuclear fission can also be used for good. Today, controlled nuclear reactions are used in power stations to produce electricity. Some people think this is a much cleaner way to produce power than stations that use coal or gas. Others worry about the radiation produced, the disposal of radioactive waste, and the possibility of accidents.

Radiation can also be used to attack some illnesses like cancer, although there are side effects that can make the patient sick, too.

9 NUCLEAR FUSION

Researchers today are conducting experiments into nuclear fission's opposite process—**NUCLEAR FUSION**. This is the type of reaction that happens in a star. They experiment with a super-hot mixture in which particles crash into each other, producing new particles and lots of energy. This reaction causes much less radioactivity and might be a safe, clean way to produce power in the future.

⑩ SMALLER PARTICLES

Scientists now think that some tiny particles are themselves made of even tinier particles. These tiny particles have unusual names like **QUARKS**, **ANTIQUARKS**, **BOSONS**, and **LEPTONS**. They are as small as electrons and have their own characteristics.
In 2008, the CERN research center on the border between French and Switzerland opened the Large Hadron Collider. This is a giant laboratory for thousands of scientists from around the world. A huge tunnel, 17 miles long, is used to conduct experiments that mirror the moments right after the Big Bang. This allows them to study how subatomic particles behave and to discover brand-new particles, too.

MEDICINE

For as long as humans have existed, they have fought illness and injury. But doctors and modern medicine have only really started to understand the human body and the causes of poor health relatively recently. Today, there are many medical inventions that help us to prevent illness, but 250 years ago, none of these existed at all.

1 ANCIENT HEALERS

Medicine has been around for thousands of years. Initially, tribes had healers or shamans, and later communities relied on medicine men. These people were skilled and learned lessons from elders about how to deal with broken bones, which plants could cure which illnesses, and how to treat injuries, burns, rashes, and fevers.

As they learned more about the human body, the treatments they used became more sophisticated.

> This healing skill became a science and these healers became doctors.

2 EARLY MEDICINE

The "Father of Medicine," Hippocrates, who was born in 460 BC, taught his many students how doctors should be careful and caring when treating patients. He advised them to "first do no harm." He described the symptoms and treatments for many conditions.

In 16th century Europe, people known as **APOTHECARIES** used herbs and plants to make medicines. Many books of herbs at the time identified and described plants, and listed recipes for making remedies for headaches and stomach pains.

Around the same time, a Swiss physician, Paracelsus, examined how certain foods and medicines could actually make people ill. He discovered that the amount the patient consumed was important, and said that "the dose maketh the poison." In other words, a medicine that can be helpful in small doses can be dangerous in high doses. This finding was crucial and still just as important today: if you are prescribed medicine by your doctor, you will also be advised on the **DOSAGE**, which is how much medicine to take and how often.

> The dose maketh the poison...

3 ANATOMY

ANATOMY is the study of the structure of the human body, of our muscles, bones, and organs.

The ancient Egyptians knew about some organs because they removed them when a dead person was mummified. But they didn't know what each organ did to keep the body healthy and alive.

The ancient Greek philosopher Galen, born in the year 129, was inspired by Hippocrates's ideas to study anatomy, nerves, and muscles. He even performed eye and brain surgery.

Over the centuries, much more research into anatomy was conducted by doctors who dissected dead bodies, cutting into them to discover which parts were connected and how they might all work together.

In 15th century Italy, Leonardo da Vinci dissected bodies and made detailed drawings of what he saw in an attempt to understand the structure of muscles for his paintings.

Later, in 1628, Englishman William Harvey's studies led him to figure out that the heart powers our bodies. It pumps blood around tiny tubes called arteries and veins, in what is called the **CIRCULATORY SYSTEM**. He wrote about this in his book *De Motu Cordis*. We now understand how all our organs work, and how different types of illnesses and diseases affect our bodies.

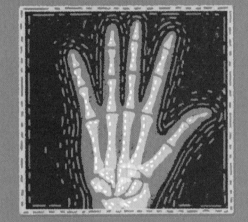

Today, we can see into bodies without cutting them open. In 1895, German physicist Wilhelm Röntgen used a newly-discovered type of radiation to create the first ever image of the inside of a body. This first medical **X-RAY** was of his wife's hand; the X-rays passed through her skin and muscles but not her bones, so the X-ray was a clear picture of the bones of her hand.

4 SURGERY

It is one thing to understand the anatomy of a body, but to try to fix or remove something that is damaged is much more complicated. To cut into a body without hurting the patient is so difficult that surgery has only been a real part of medicine for about a hundred years.

Operations were performed for centuries before that but they were always risky procedures. Patients could lose huge amounts of blood and sometimes did not survive. Doctors tried to give **BLOOD TRANSFUSIONS**—topping up a patient's body with someone else's blood—but it would not always work.

Then, in 1901, Austrian biologist Karl Landsteiner wanted to understand why this was, and he discovered that people can have different blood types. Blood types must match for transfusions to succeed.

Surgery is now safe and scientific. Surgeons train for years to learn the skills needed during surgery. They now use specialized, sharp tools in clean operating theaters.

> There is even a branch of surgery called KEYHOLE SURGERY, where a laser creates a tiny hole through which the whole operation can be conducted.

> There is ANESTHESIA to make the patient sleep and feel no pain, and machines to monitor heart rate and breathing.

⑤ PAINKILLERS

Medicine has come a long way from healers mixing potions. As well as curing a patient's symptoms, doctors are now also able to offer them relief from their symptoms with **PAINKILLERS**.

In 1897, the German chemist Felix Hoffman, working at the Bayer company, developed a man-made version of a medicine that healers had extracted from the bark of willow trees for thousands of years. These tablets were the first commercial aspirin, a very effective painkiller.

Today, chemists have developed many kinds of painkillers—some mild, some very strong. All of them work by acting on our nervous systems to stop our brains from registering pain.

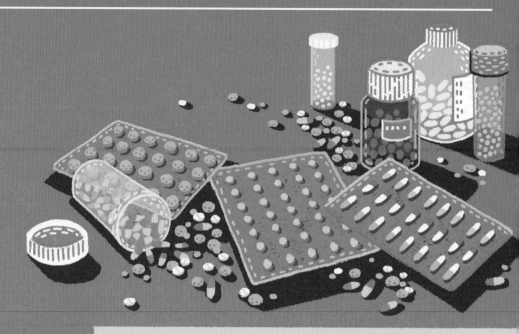

⑥ ANESTHETICS

Imagine having surgery while you are still awake, and you can feel everything that is happening...Well, for people living just under a few hundred years ago, that was exactly what happened!

It was not until 1847 that the Scotsman Dr. James Simpson discovered that if patients inhaled the fumes from a liquid called chloroform before an operation they would sleep through the procedure. This was the first **ANESTHESIA** and it made a big difference to patients who no longer had to experience the terror—and agony—of surgery.

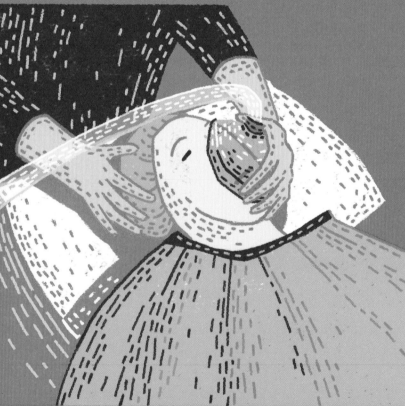

Today, doctors are able to use two kinds of anesthetics. General anesthetics put the patient to sleep for a short while, making them completely unconscious during an operation. Local anesthetics are used for smaller procedures, like getting stitches or having a tooth removed. They don't put the patient to sleep and only stop the sensation in one part of their body for a while, so even though you can see the stitches being put in, you can't feel a thing.

⑦ GERMS

Diseases were a big part of life in the ancient and medieval world, and whole continents were ravaged by plagues that could kill millions of people at a time. While many people looked to religion for answers, others wondered what caused the illnesses.

Doctors eventually realized that a high body temperature is a sign of illness. The invention of the **THERMOMETER** allowed them to check if a patient had a fever. Early types of thermometers were known as **THERMOSCOPES** and were invented in 16th century Venice by the physician Santorio Santorii.

In the 1860s, doctors in Europe and North America began to understand how people became ill. The theory of **GERMS**—the idea that small, microscopic creatures could carry diseases—was developed. Doctors also realized that unhygienic surroundings allowed diseases to spread easily, and the introduction of proper sewage systems in cities made people much healthier.

> By diagnosing the source of different illnesses (the infection, the virus, the bacteria) researchers have developed medicines based on plants and chemicals that find and start fighting it, without damaging healthy parts of the body.

8 ANTIBIOTICS

One of the biggest medical breakthroughs happened in 1928. Scottish biologist Alexander Fleming discovered a new medicine—the first **ANTIBIOTIC**: penicillin. Antibiotics attack the bacteria that cause many dangerous diseases.

Thanks to antibiotics, treating wounds and performing surgery became much safer for the patient, and many people that before would have died from infections caused by their injuries could now survive. The arrival of antibiotics came as many soldiers were wounded in the Second World War, and saved many thousands of lives.

Several families of antibiotics have since been developed by chemists, making it quite uncommon for people to die of infections, when before it was a major cause of death around the world. However, over time, bacteria can evolve, becoming resistant to particular antibiotics. Today, scientists are in a race to develop new antibiotics to combat different strains of bacteria.

9 VACCINES

In 1796, English scientist Edward Jenner developed the first ever **VACCINE**. He gave his first patient, a young boy, a small dose of a disease called cowpox. This allowed his body to recognize the infection and gave his immune system a head start in fighting it so that when he came into contact with a stronger disease, smallpox, his body knew how to deal with that infection, too.

This was a huge leap forward in medicine. Today, doctors can protect people from more than 25 diseases, including polio, measles, and tetanus. Smallpox—which was a horrible illness that covered the sufferer in boils and gave them a high fever—has been wiped out altogether.

Researchers are still trying to develop new vaccines to combat other life-threatening illnesses, like cancer.

10 DNA

Scientists knew that there had to be a chemical code inside humans, programming how our cells and bodies grow, live, and look. In 1950s England, Maurice Wilkins and Rosalind Franklin were able to use X-rays to generate an image of a sample of **DNA**. This allowed the biologists James Watson and Francis Crick to study its structure. They discovered that DNA is made of two twisted, linked chains of chemicals.

DNA stands for deoxyribonucleic acid. It lives in the heart of each of our cells and it is responsible for who we are: the fact that we look like our family, that we have a certain eye and hair color, and that we inherit some diseases. It is a blueprint that carries genetic information from one generation to the next.

Today, scientists can analyze patients' DNA to discover what is going on in their cells and whether they might have any genetic coding that could make them more likely to become ill. This allows doctors to work out what treatment and medicine would work best for their patients. We now know that DNA is as individual as a fingerprint: the only two people to have exactly the same DNA are identical twins. This means DNA samples can be used to identify criminals in police investigations and to trace family trees. Understanding DNA can also help researchers study inherited medical conditions and develop new treatments.

MATERIALS

The world we live in today looks very different than that of our ancestors. Architects design huge concrete skyscrapers, engineers create machines from metal, buildings are filled with plastic products, and people carry complex technology in their very own pockets. All of this is possible because of chemists' understanding of materials.

1 MATERIALS AND SUBSTANCES

MATTER is anything that has weight and takes up space. It is the name scientists give to all the stuff in our universe. It can exist in different states: solid, liquid, and gas. Matter is made of atoms but they are so tiny that we cannot see them around us. However, what we can see, use, feel, build, and make things from, are MATERIALS and SUBSTANCES. Wood, stone, glass, and metals are examples of materials. Liquids, like shampoo, gases, like air, and plastics are all types of substances.

Materials and substances are really useful in everyday life. Just like people have personalities, materials and substances have properties. Their properties are how they look, feel, and behave—and these make them suitable for certain jobs and unsuitable for others.

2 PROPERTIES OF MATERIALS

Materials have different characteristics that make them useful for different purposes. These characteristics are known as the PROPERTIES of the materials.

Today, the study of materials, and the design of new ones—MATERIALS SCIENCE—is considered an important area of science and engineering, as much of our technological advancements depend on the materials available to us.

These are some of the most important properties that different materials can have:

Waterproof   Absorbent   Strong

3 METALS

Early humans mostly used stone and wood because they were easy to find, but they also made crude tools from pieces of **METAL** elements they discovered.

Our earliest ancestors didn't know how to create or use fire. The first flames they saw were probably caused by bolts of lightning! But eventually humans learned how to start fires themselves around 350,000 years ago—probably by striking stones together. By using fire, they found they could extract more metal from rocks called **ORES**. They also discovered they could heat metals, making them soft. From around 5,500 BC, they molded the metal to make more

sophisticated tools and weapons. Then metal workers found that instead of using just one metal, they could melt copper and tin together to create a new, stronger metal: bronze. This was the start of the **BRONZE AGE**, which began in such regions as Greece and China around 3,000 BC, and in Britain in 2,000 BC.

The most important form of metal technology discovered was iron. Widespread use of iron, which signaled the beginning of the **IRON AGE**, began between 1,200 BC to 600 BC, depending on the region of the world. Iron continues to be the most widely-used metal today.

It's likely the iron was sourced from meteorites that had fallen to Earth.

Iron is thought to have first been used by the ancient Egyptians as far back as around 3,200 BC.

The early Middle Ages was a time when much of the knowledge and scientific theories of the ancient world were lost and forgotten. During this time, a mixture of science and magic called ALCHEMY was popular. Alchemists thought that they could mysteriously change dull metals into shiny gold, and that they could create potions that would make them eternally young. However, during their experiments, they also discovered many genuinely useful chemical processes and reactions. In many ways, alchemy was a predecessor of modern chemistry.

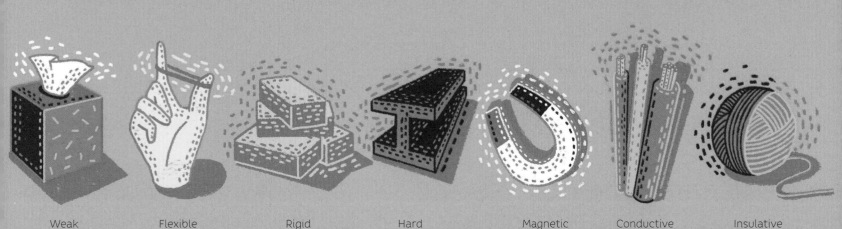

Weak   Flexible   Rigid   Hard   Magnetic   Conductive   Insulative

4 GLASS

The first **GLASS** was created naturally, when sand was superheated by lightning strikes or volcanic lava. These rare pieces of glass were found and used as ornaments by ancient civilizations.

Then ancient metal workers in Mesopotamia started to discover that small glass beads could sometimes be created as a by-product of **SMELTING** metals in hot fires. By the 3rd century BC, large workshops in India were making glass from sand and creating molten glass in very hot fires. They would pour it into molds to create jewelry and household objects.

Around 200 years later, a new technique, called **GLASS-BLOWING** was developed and used by the Romans. This glass was created by sticking a blowpipe into molten glass and inflating the glass like a balloon, while rolling it to give it shape. Later, a similar technique was used in medieval Europe.

In 1959, Alastair Pilkington developed a new technique of making glass: float glass. By pouring the molten glass on molten metal, he could create huge, flat sheets of glass of the same thickness. Architects were now able to create buildings made with enormous glass windows, and the skylines of our cities changed forever.

5 CHEMISTRY

Jābir ibn Hayyān, born in 721, was a Persian scientist. He conducted serious experiments, studied many chemicals and their reactions, and recorded all his findings in a logical, analytical way.

During the late 17th and 18th centuries, in a time known as **THE ENLIGHTENMENT**, people began to think about the world around them in a more inquisitive way. There were political revolutions as well as new ideas about society, the arts, and culture. Science changed, too. New theories were shared and scholars discussed and wrote about how experiments should be conducted.

Whereas before this time, scientists had been called "natural philosophers," the public now began to read papers about experiments and became interested in learning how science affected their lives. The title "scientist" was widely used and, at last, it was seen as a real profession. Some researchers, like the Englishman Michael Faraday and the American Benjamin Franklin, even became celebrities.

Irishman Robert Boyle pioneered the new, precise science of chemicals—chemistry—in his book *The Sceptical Chymist* of 1661. He said that substances react together to produce new substances; they are not mystically changed from one material to another.

Across Europe in the 18th century, chemists made a number of important discoveries. In Scotland, Joseph Black studied the gas produced when limestone reacts with acid. He knew that this was heavier than air, that a fire would not burn in it and that it was the same gas that animals breathed out. He had discovered **CARBON DIOXIDE**.

Carl Wilhelm Scheele in Sweden and Joseph Priestley in England both conducted their own experiments into a gas produced by reactions involving a chemical called mercury oxide. They noticed that the gas made fires burn brighter and was easy to breathe. They had discovered **OXYGEN**.

And, in England, Henry Cavendish studied the reactions between different metals and strong acids, and noticed a gas produced by these reactions. He had discovered **HYDROGEN**.

6 EXPLOSIVES

Chemical reactions happen when chemicals are combined together and their atoms rearrange to produce new chemicals, called **PRODUCTS**.

One of the most important types of reaction is **COMBUSTION**. This is what happens when something burns and produces heat and sometimes smoke. Some substances combust very quickly, burning violently and causing an explosion as well as heat and smoke. These substances are called **EXPLOSIVES**.

Alchemists in 8th century China, who were trying to develop a potion for eternal life, instead created a powerfully explosive powder: **GUNPOWDER**. This was one of the earliest explosives and was used in the first fireworks and weapons. Some elements burn with colored flames, and when a firework explodes, it burns with the color of the main chemical ingredient—creating the brightly colored sparks we see in the sky.

Much later, in 18th century France, Antoine Lavoisier studied water, oxygen, hydrogen, and combustion reactions. He invented different explosives and wrote the first ever chemistry textbook.

⑦ CONSUMER CHEMISTRY

Our modern lives are full of chemicals. If chemists, inventors, and chemical engineers had not calculated how to make chemicals react together to create new materials, substances and plastics, our world would be a very different place.

In 1935, Wallace Carothers worked with a team of research chemists at a company called DuPont to create a new material called **NYLON**. It was soon used to make the bristles of toothbrushes as well as parachutes, tents, ropes, stockings, and tights.

We rely on chemicals not only for the fabric of the clothes we wear, but also the colors of those fabrics and the detergents they're washed with. When we use toothpaste, mouthwash, shampoo, and soap, chemicals are cleaning our bodies. Some of the food we eat is kept fresh by gases used during packaging. And when we are sick and take medication, chemicals in the medicine are helping our immune systems to fight off the illness.

⑧ PLASTICS

PLASTICS are man-made substances that come from raw materials like oil and gas, using processes that have been invented in research labs. The first plastics were invented in the late 19th century but it was not until the 20th century that scientists realized how they could be mass-produced, and what uses they might have.

Plastics can be dyed different colors and molded into different shapes. Some plastics are soft, like those used for shopping bags and waterproof clothing, while others are hard—like those used to make bottles, packaging, and toys.

During the 1900s in America, Leo Baekeland created the first widely-used hard, moldable plastic, **BAKELITE**. It was soon used for kitchenware, jewelry, pipes, toys, and weapons. His invention was the beginning of the "age of plastics."

In 1938, another American, Roy J. Plunkett, discovered a waxy solid by accident. It was extremely heat-resistant and nonstick, and was later named **TEFLON**. It would soon be used in cables, weatherproof clothing, and frying pans.

A plastic called **MYLAR** was invented by DuPont and NASA when they were developing lightweight materials to take into space. It is used for "space blankets," which are also given to exhausted marathon runners, and to people suffering from exposure.

KEVLAR is a man-made material that was invented by Stephanie Kwolek and her team at DuPont in 1965. It is extremely strong and traps bullets in its fibers. It is used today to make bulletproof helmets and vests, as well as sports protection gear.

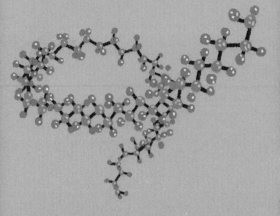

Plastics are made of giant molecules called POLYMERS that have thousands of carbon and hydrogen atoms linked together in long chains.

9 RECYCLING

Plastics allow us to make lots of objects that would be impossible to make in other materials. However, plastics do not decompose in the same way as materials such as paper or wood. When we throw away a plastic bag, it does not rot in the ground—it might take a thousand years to break down. That is why it is important to RECYCLE plastics as often as possible so that we do not pollute the planet.

Recycling starts with you! You throw your waste plastic, glass, paper, and tin into the recycling bin.

It is taken to a recycling plant.

It is then processed, sorted, and compressed into bales.

The plastic bale is ground into small parts and washed.

This process creates recycled plastic fibers...

...that can be used to create new products.

10 NANOTECHNOLOGY

In comparison to the wood, glass, stone, and metals that humans have been using for thousands of years, plastics have only been around for about 100 years—so they are still relatively new. But scientists are already busy developing the future of material science—NANOTECHNOLOGY.

Anything nanoscopic is really, really tiny—1,000 times smaller than microscopic objects, which can be seen under a regular microscope. Nanotechnology deals with the design and use of materials on an extremely small scale.

Jack Kilby was the American engineer who developed the first INTEGRATED CIRCUIT, also known as the MICROCHIP, while working at a company called Texas Instruments.

A chip is made of a material called SILICON. Lots of electronic circuits can be created on one single chip. This allows computers to become faster and smaller, and for gadgets to be invented that are actually tiny, portable computers.

Other nanotechnologies are being developed to help build nanochips for ultra-small computer components. NANOMACHINES clean up pollution, while CARBON NANOTUBES—tiny, hollow tubes built from tightly-packed carbon atoms—could be used to deliver drug molecules directly to a human cell.

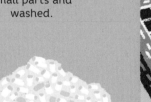

ENERGY

The universe is driven by energy. It exists in many states—it can be stored for thousands of years, or it can power movement. By understanding how to transform natural energy into electrical power, scientists have created a world that glows so brightly, you can see our biggest cities from space at night.

① KINDS OF ENERGY

ENERGY is the ability to move and do work. It turns wheels and powers machines. It can be provided by a person, by heat, by wind, by water, or by electricity. Energy exists in different forms:

THERMAL ENERGY (HEAT)
This is created by atoms or molecules moving or vibrating.

POTENTIAL ENERGY AND GRAVITATIONAL ENERGY
Any object can have potential—or stored—energy. Gravitational energy has to do with the position of the object: the higher from the ground an object is held, like a ball, the more gravitational energy it has.

RADIANT ENERGY
This is the energy of electromagnetic waves. Light is a form of radiant energy.

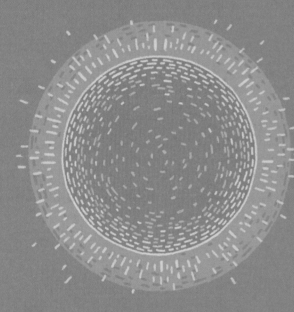

KINETIC ENERGY (MOTION)
Anything that moves—from a swinging pendulum to a traveling planet—has kinetic energy.

ELECTRICAL ENERGY
This is created by the movement of charged particles, like protons or electrons.

MECHANICAL ENERGY
This combines an object's kinetic energy with its potential energy. A hammer hitting a nail has mechanical energy, which combines the potential energy of the hammer up in the air with the kinetic energy as it moves through the air.

CHEMICAL ENERGY
This is stored in the bonds of chemical compounds and is released when the bonds break down in a chemical reaction. Often, this reaction creates heat and other kinds of energy as a by-product (as in an explosion).

SOUND ENERGY
This is a kind of mechanical energy. Sound energy is created when an object vibrates and sound waves travel through the air.

② TRANSFORMING ENERGY

Energy can be used and changed into different kinds, but it never disappears. For most of human history, we have used natural, readily available sources of energy. We have used water and wind to power machines, and people and animals to pull carts, levers, and pulleys. Energy can be transformed several times over into different kinds of energy.

The sun shines and its RADIANT ENERGY hits the surface of the Earth.

The grass uses the radiant energy to make food from the sunlight, transforming it into CHEMICAL ENERGY.

A horse eats grass. As it digests the food, it transfers the chemical energy stored in the grass into MECHANICAL ENERGY, which allows it to move.

The horse might carry out mechanical work, and pull a carriage.

As the carriage speeds up, it gains KINETIC ENERGY.

③ POWERING ENGINES

An **ENGINE** is a machine that changes one type of energy into mechanical energy—motion.

It wasn't until the 18th century that scientists discovered sources of energy, such as chemical energy, which could power an engine.

A heat engine burns fuel to create heat (or thermal energy). The heat then creates a push—a mechanical motion. Types of heat engines include steam engines, internal combustion engines, and electric motors. Between 1760 and 1780, James Watt designed a successful steam engine in Scotland—one of the first kinds of heat engine. In the 19th century, steam power drove the Industrial Revolution.

1. Coal was burned, transforming its CHEMICAL ENERGY into THERMAL ENERGY.

2. The THERMAL ENERGY boiled the water into steam.

3. The steam then did the mechanical work to force the pistons to move up and down.

4. As the wheels drove forward, the locomotive had KINETIC ENERGY.

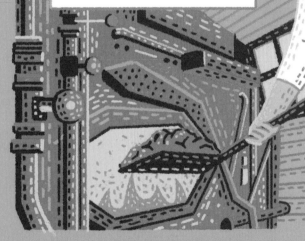

④ STATIC ELECTRICITY

There are two types of electricity: **STATIC** and **CURRENT**. Static electricity comes from the buildup of the negative charges carried by electrons. The charges gather on the surface of an object, and when enough charge exists, a **DISCHARGE**, or shock, happens. This is the type of electricity that occurs during a lightning storm or when a metal door handle shocks you.

American polymath Benjamin Franklin was interested in electricity and experimented with lightning—which is a bolt of natural electricity. In 1752 he flew a kite, attached to a key, during a storm. The lightning was attracted to the metal key and struck it. Buildings now have lightning rods because metal allows electricity to flow safely through it. Metal is what is known as a **CONDUCTOR**.

1. Up in a thundercloud, droplets of frozen rain move around and bump into each other, causing an electrical charge to build up.

2. The positive charge rises to the top of the cloud and the negative charge sinks to the bottom of the cloud.

3. The negative charge causes an opposite, positive charge to build up on the ground below. The positive charge reaches up toward the cloud from tall objects, like a tree or a church spire.

4. When the negative charge of the cloud connects with the positive charge of a tree, a lightning bolt is produced.

⑤ DIRECT CURRENT ELECTRICITY

CURRENT electricity comes from the movement, or flow, of electrons. This is the type that we generate in a power station. It is supplied to buildings through wires or stored in batteries. When we plug an appliance in, or charge our gadgets, we use electricity to power our modern lives.

Electricity is caused by electrons. Electrons carry negative charge, and when they flow through a metal wire from a battery or socket, they create an electrical current. A circuit is a complete loop of wire that the electrons can travel around. The current powers things around the circuit, like lightbulbs or household appliances.

There are two types of electrical current: **DIRECT CURRENT** and **ALTERNATING CURRENT**. The first to be discovered was direct current: electricity that flows in one direction.

Italian physicist Alessandro Volta invented the first battery around 1800. It was called a **VOLTAIC PILE** and was made of layers of discs of copper and zinc sandwiched between pieces of paper that had been soaked in salty water. When a piece of copper wire linked the top and bottom of the battery, a current flowed. The unit for measuring electricity is named **VOLT** in his honor. Direct current electricity is still found in batteries today.

Electrons flow from the negative terminal of the BATTERY to the positive terminal

The BULB is lit by the electrical current

An electrical current flows through the COPPER WIRES

6 ALTERNATING CURRENT ELECTRICITY

Serbian-American inventor Nikola Tesla discovered the second type of electrical current, ALTERNATING CURRENT, in 1887. This flowed in one direction and then reversed and flowed back in the opposite direction, many times a minute. Alternating current electricity is used in the electricity that travels to our buildings through cables and wires.

An influential inventor at the time, Thomas Edison, had invested all his time and money into making direct current electricity the electricity that the public would use. Yet it could not be easily adapted to different voltages for different uses. Tesla believed that alternating current electricity was more efficient and was the future of the electrification of homes and cities.

In the 1880s, the two men and their companies had a long, pubic argument called "The War of the Currents." They fought about who was right, which power supply was better, cheaper, and safer. Eventually alternating current electricity won the argument and is now the current used around the world.

7 GENERATING ELECTRICITY

3. The current then flows to a TRANSFORMER, which alters the strength of the current—the VOLTAGE—before it travels to buildings.

4. The current leaves the factory in large, long metal cables, which carry it to houses, offices, towns, and cities. When the current reaches a building, it flows through metal wires inside the walls as mains electricity.

2. This energy moves a piece of equipment called a GENERATOR. It spins a huge magnet inside coils of wire, to produce an electric current.

5. We can use the electricity by plugging appliances, like TVs and computers, into the walls' electrical sockets.

1. Electricity is generated in huge factories called POWER STATIONS. Coal, gas, oil, biomass, or nuclear fuels are used to produce heat energy.

8 ELECTROMAGNETISM

When a magnet spins inside a coil of wire, an electric current is generated. When a current flows, a magnetic field is created. This behavior is called **ELECTROMAGNETISM**. An electromagnet is a kind of temporary magnet—it is magnetic when the current flows, but ceases to be when the current stops.

Hans Christian Ørsted and André-Marie Ampère both investigated the relationship between magnets and electricity in the 18th and 19th centuries, and Michael Faraday studied electricity and electromagnetism at a similar time. He gave public lectures to tell people about his findings. He created an early electric motor and invented a piece of equipment called a Faraday cage, which allows electricity workers today to stay safe from electrocution.

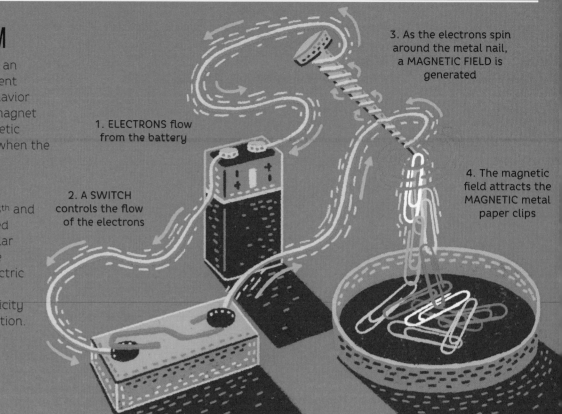

3. As the electrons spin around the metal nail, a MAGNETIC FIELD is generated

1. ELECTRONS flow from the battery

2. A SWITCH controls the flow of the electrons

4. The magnetic field attracts the MAGNETIC metal paper clips

9 FOSSIL FUELS

Many of the things humans use to produce heat energy are called **FOSSIL FUELS**. Fossil fuels are made of animal and plant matter that have died millions of years ago, and have decomposed, buried deep underground. They contain chemical energy, and there are three kinds: **OIL**, **NATURAL GAS**, and **COAL**.

In the 19th century, there were already fears that we would run out of fossil fuels. There is only so much of this kind of fuel on Earth—it is not possible to create more. Another huge problem with fossil fuels is that by burning them to release their energy, we also produce gases that damage the environment, such as an excess of carbon dioxide. A buildup of these gases, known as **GREENHOUSE GASES**, is trapping the heat in our atmosphere that would otherwise escape. This is causing the Earth's surface temperature to rise in a phenomenon known as **GLOBAL WARMING**.

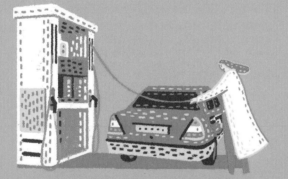

OIL—or petroleum—is a sticky black liquid that is sucked out of the ground from oil wells. From this, we get the fuel that powers cars and planes, as well as some power plants.

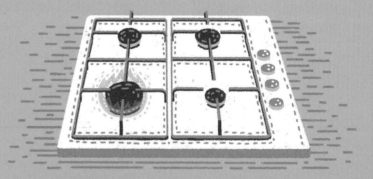

NATURAL GAS—mostly made up of methane—is a chemical compound lighter than air. Pipes supply gas to our homes, powering our central heating and gas stoves.

COAL is a black rock, mined from the earth. Coal was burned to create the steam that powered the machines of the Industrial Revolution and is still used in power stations and in fireplaces today.

NUCLEAR POWER uses nuclear fission to produce energy from elements such as uranium.

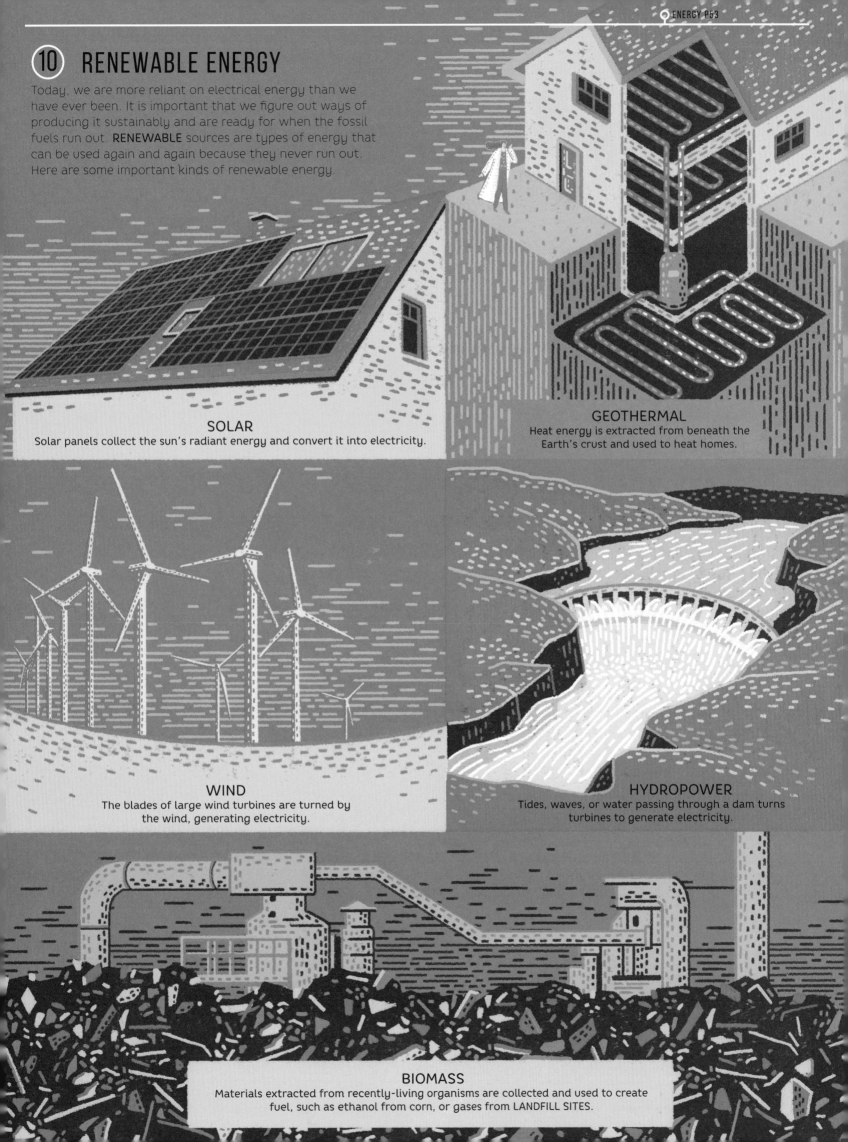

⑩ RENEWABLE ENERGY

Today, we are more reliant on electrical energy than we have ever been. It is important that we figure out ways of producing it sustainably and are ready for when the fossil fuels run out. RENEWABLE sources are types of energy that can be used again and again because they never run out. Here are some important kinds of renewable energy.

SOLAR
Solar panels collect the sun's radiant energy and convert it into electricity.

GEOTHERMAL
Heat energy is extracted from beneath the Earth's crust and used to heat homes.

WIND
The blades of large wind turbines are turned by the wind, generating electricity.

HYDROPOWER
Tides, waves, or water passing through a dam turns turbines to generate electricity.

BIOMASS
Materials extracted from recently-living organisms are collected and used to create fuel, such as ethanol from corn, or gases from LANDFILL SITES.

LIFE

Earth is at just the right distance from the sun to support life. It isn't too hot or too cold—it's a Goldilocks planet, with perfect conditions for things to live. The heat, together with our oxygen-rich atmosphere, means that life flourishes here. Scientists believe that life started as tiny microscopic creatures on Earth about 4 billion years ago.

1 LIVING THINGS

Classifying things into "living" or "dead" may seem like a straightforward, obvious way of looking at the world, but in fact it is not always straightforward to tell whether an object is living or not. Is a barnacle a living thing? Is lichen alive?

The first people to think about the natural world in this way were the ancient Greeks—Aristotle, in particular, was interested in the diversity of living things.

Today, the definition of what makes something a living thing is still being argued over by scientists, but most agree that the following factors are shared by anything that is alive:

NUTRITION
Anything living must take in energy to stay alive: animals eat food and plants absorb the sun's energy.

EXCRETION
The water that is produced through respiration is a by-product that isn't needed by the living thing—so it is excreted. The same thing happens when animals eat food—the waste is excreted as poop.

RESPIRATION
In this chemical reaction, living things combine oxygen and sugars to release water, carbon dioxide, and energy. Animals do this by breathing. In plants, respiration is the opposite of photosynthesis.

RESPONSE
Living things respond to their environment, to seek out food or avoid danger. Plants send down roots for water and reach up to the sunlight.

MOVEMENT
All animals and plants are able to move, whether they walk, open their shells, or track the light.

REPRODUCTION
All living things are able to produce offspring. This can happen in diverse ways, from giving birth or laying eggs, to dispersing spores or seeds.

GROWTH
All living things change shape as they grow older, usually getting bigger in size.

② CLASSIFICATION

Aristotle's scrutiny of living things led him to write a book in the 4th century BC called *History of Animals*. He classified 500 different types of birds, mammals, and fish in the book, and related them to each other in a "ladder of life."

Hundreds of years later, in 1735, Swedish scientist Carl Linnaeus developed Aristotle's classification of animals. He used a system called **TAXONOMY** to define and name animals by groups, based on their shared characteristics—such as their bodily features and ways of reproducing.

In 1879, in Germany, Ernst Haeckel drew a complex illustration to show how all life-forms on Earth are connected. It was called **THE TREE OF LIFE**. Zoologists have continued to refine this diagram and today The Tree of Life shows all animals separated into two groups: **VERTEBRATES**, which have a backbone, and **INVERTEBRATES**, which do not.

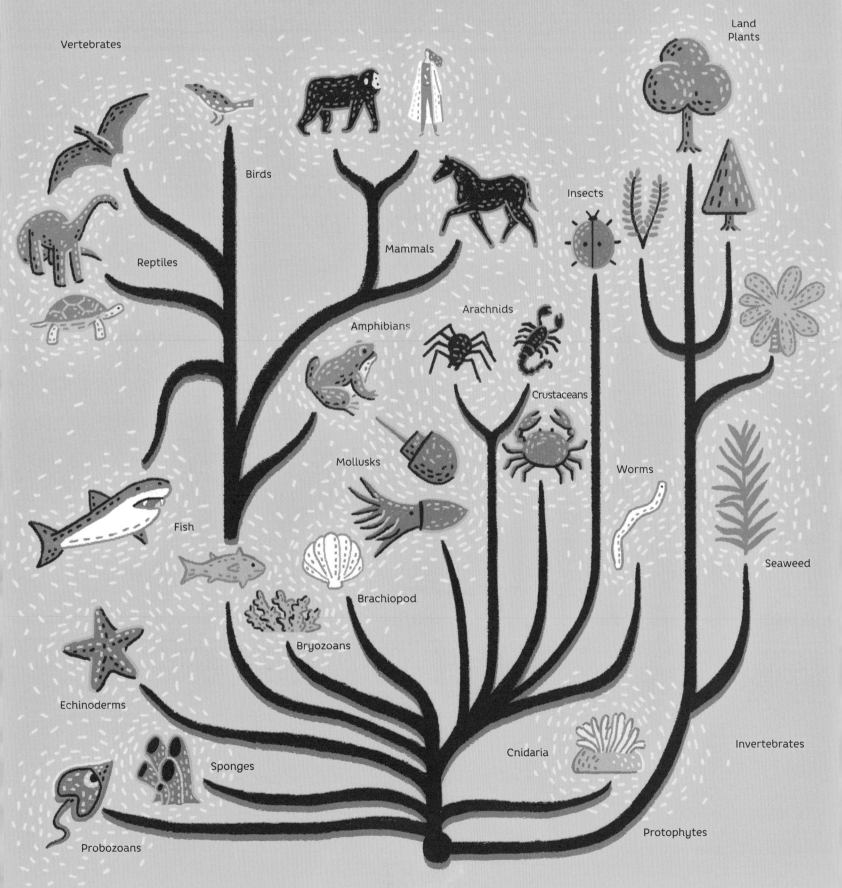

Vertebrates

Land Plants

Birds

Insects

Reptiles

Mammals

Arachnids

Amphibians

Crustaceans

Mollusks

Worms

Fish

Seaweed

Brachiopod

Bryozoans

Echinoderms

Cnidaria

Invertebrates

Sponges

Protophytes

Probozoans

③ EVOLUTION

In 1831, a young English naturalist called Charles Darwin set sail on a world voyage on board HMS *Beagle*. Over the next five years, he would see four continents, study hundreds of animals, conduct research, and collect specimens. On different islands in the Galapagos, he saw slightly different species of finches and tortoises, and began to wonder why they were similar but also had certain traits suited to life in their own habitats. These ideas would eventually help him develop his theory of **EVOLUTION**, which he set out in his book, *On the Origin of Species*.

Darwin proposed that all the different species on Earth are descended from simple life-forms that gradually changed over the generations. He believed that a system called **NATURAL SELECTION** governed these changes. It is sometimes called "the survival of the fittest" and it means that the species or individuals with the strongest and most suitable characteristics for survival in their environment are the most likely to do well and reproduce. They pass these advantages on to their children, and each generation becomes stronger and more suited to their habitat.

Darwin's theory is supported by a great deal of research that he conducted, as well as evidence that has since been collected. For example, **FOSSILS** (stone imprints of bones from ancient animals) show that today's horses have evolved slowly from a horse-like, dog-size creature that lived 60 million years ago.

Many groups disagreed with Darwin's theories: they held rallies and lectures to share their opinions publicly. These scientists and religious groups thought human life did not evolve but developed in different ways. However, today, zoologists hold Darwin's revolutionary theory of evolution to be true.

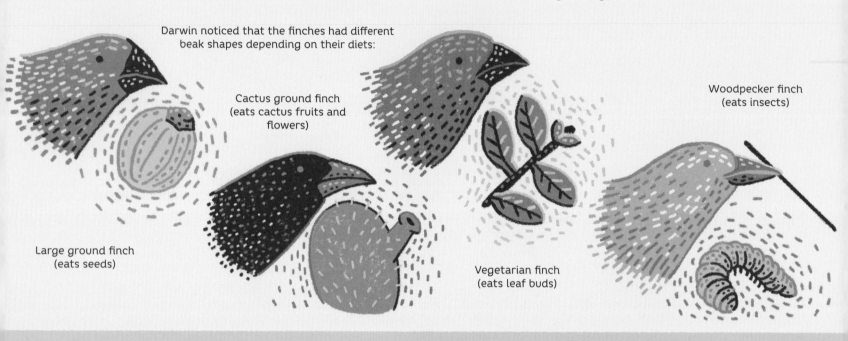

Darwin noticed that the finches had different beak shapes depending on their diets:

Cactus ground finch (eats cactus fruits and flowers)

Woodpecker finch (eats insects)

Large ground finch (eats seeds)

Vegetarian finch (eats leaf buds)

④ ORIGINS OF HUMANKIND

Evolution also explains how apes and humans have common ancestors—we belong to different branches of the primate family tree. In fact, DNA evidence shows that human and chimpanzee DNA matches by 98 percent!

Around 200,000 years ago, human ancestor apes evolved into two different types of early human—*Homo sapiens* and *Homo neanderthalensis*. *Homo sapiens* had more complicated brains suited to creativity and communication, which helped with tribal life, so they thrived—while the Neanderthals died out 20,000 years ago. We are *Homo sapiens*.

Between 1967 and 1974, during an archaeological dig in Ethiopia, some very ancient bones were found.

They were named the **OMO REMAINS.** Later testing showed that some of them were the oldest *Homo sapiens* remains ever discovered. They are around 195,000 years old, so scientists think that human life evolved first in Africa, with groups then migrating around the world.

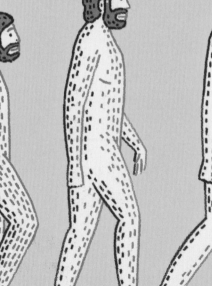

⑤ CELLS

All living things, from huge whales to tiny microorganisms, contain biological building blocks called **CELLS**. You have about 10 trillion cells in your body. There are lots of different types, including blood, brain, skin, and muscle cells; they all do different jobs. Similar cells work together to form **TISSUES** like muscles, and many tissues together form **ORGANS**, such as the heart. Lots of organs working together make up **ORGANISMS**.

The first cell was discovered in 1663 by Robert Hooke, when he looked at samples of a cork plant under a microscope. More than 170 years later, in 1839, German scientists Theodor Schwann and Matthias Jakob Schleiden described **CELL THEORY**—the idea that every living thing is made entirely from cells.

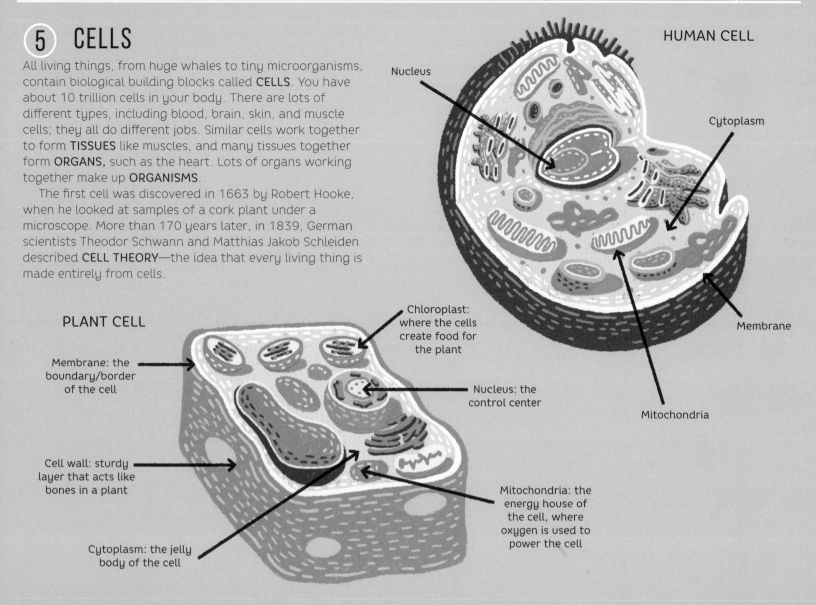

HUMAN CELL

Nucleus

Cytoplasm

Membrane

Mitochondria

PLANT CELL

Membrane: the boundary/border of the cell

Chloroplast: where the cells create food for the plant

Nucleus: the control center

Cell wall: sturdy layer that acts like bones in a plant

Mitochondria: the energy house of the cell, where oxygen is used to power the cell

Cytoplasm: the jelly body of the cell

⑥ MICROORGANISMS

Also in the 1660s, in the Netherlands, Antonie van Leeuwenhoek used a microscope to examine biological samples from humans and animals. He discovered single-celled creatures called **MICROORGANISMS**.

Microorganisms are microscopic living things, which are in the air all around us. **VIRUSES**, **BACTERIA**, and **FUNGI** are all types of microorganisms

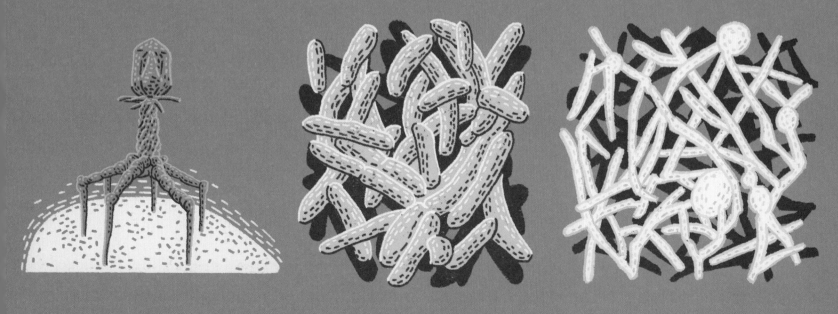

VIRUS

BACTERIA

FUNGI

⑦ GENETICS

Between 1856 and 1863, the scientist Gregor Mendel studied generations of pea plants to see which traits were passed on from parents to offspring. He became knows as the "Father of Modern Genetics."

In the heart of every cell is the nucleus—a control center. This is in charge of the cell's lifespan and activity. It is also where DNA is stored. **GENES** are sections of DNA that form biological codes. The genes use their codes to make different proteins for certain jobs in our bodies, like making us grow or giving us a certain hair color.

We receive half of our genes from one parent and half from the other, and together they make us who we are. These genes affect how we look, how tall we might be, what our personalities are like, and what diseases we might develop. This passing on of traits from parent to child is called **HEREDITY**. The science of heredity is called **GENETICS** because the code for this inheritance is passed through the DNA found in genes.

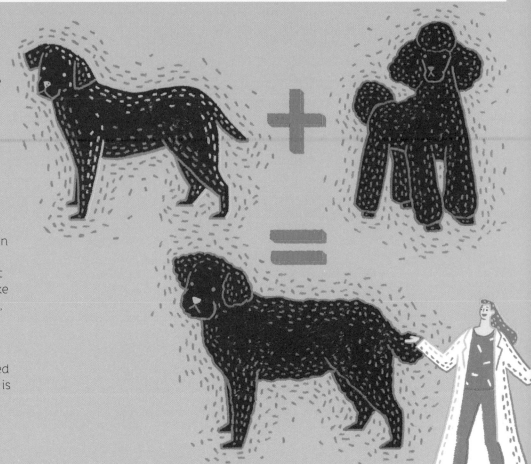

Labrador + poodle = labradoodle

⑧ THE HUMAN GENOME PROJECT

Scientists began to look closely at DNA in the mid 19th and early 20th centuries. Although James Watson and Francis Crick had already discovered the double helix structure of DNA in the 1950s, scientists now began to understand that mistakes, or **MUTATIONS**, in DNA cause medical problems. These medical problems could be **HERITABLE** between parents and their children.

In 1990, an international research program called **THE HUMAN GENOME PROJECT** was launched. Genetics scientists wanted to map all the different types of human genes. Together this map is called the **GENOME**. It is like a manual about how humans operate and where things go wrong when we get sick.

By analyzing lots of DNA samples and finding out the DNA sequence of each type of gene, scientists hoped they would find new ways to identify diseases. The genome was fully decoded in 2003 and researchers think it will help them diagnose diseases more quickly and discover ways to treat them on a cellular level.

⑨ ECOLOGY

In the 1660s, biologists began discussing the animal and plant worlds in terms of population and food chains, thinking about how groups of life-forms interact and depend on one another. It was in 1866 that Ernst Haeckel first used the word **ECOLOGY** to describe the relationship between animals, plants, and their environments.

A community of living things—the animals, plants, microorganisms—and the place or habitat they live in is called an **ECOSYSTEM**. We are all connected in a giant ecosystem. We are linked to each other and our lives affect the lives of the animals and plants around us in positive and negative ways. Animals eat other animals or plants. If those animals or plants become sick or extinct, those that eat them will be in danger, too.

Ecology is the study of ecosystems, how they behave and how the relationships within them work. The population levels and the **FOOD CHAINS** within an ecosystem may change over time, and ecologists monitor the environment to check whether it is healthy or under stress from pollution, weather, or human interference.

A food chain links animals together by showing what each one eats to survive. At the bottom of most food chains is a **HERBIVORE**, which eats grass and vegetation. At the top of the food chain is the **APEX PREDATOR**, which hunts other animals—and nothing hunts it in return.

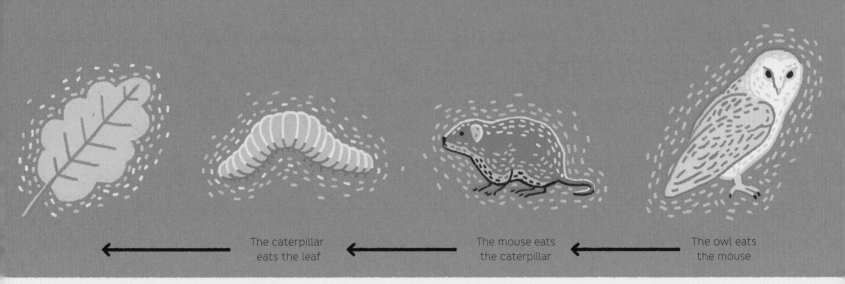

← The caterpillar eats the leaf

← The mouse eats the caterpillar

← The owl eats the mouse

⑩ ENVIRONMENTALISM

The more scientists understand ecology, the more clearly they can see the impact that humans have had on the planet: the power we produce, the chemicals we use, and the trash we throw away all affect the environment.

During the 1980s, research scientists working in Antarctica discovered that a hole was developing in the part of our atmosphere called the **OZONE LAYER**. This layer protects us from the sun's harmful rays, and it was being destroyed by the damaging chemicals produced by lots of industries. The chemicals were also contributing to the greenhouse gases in our atmosphere, adding to the problem of global warming. Governments banned the use of these pollutants and further damage to the ozone layer was limited, although it will take a long time for the layer to recover.

Now we know that humans have damaged our giant, worldwide ecosystem for centuries. But scientists are now thinking about ways to reduce pollutants, recycle our waste, and use renewable energy sources so that we can conserve our environment and keep our planet healthy.

When the last of a species of animals dies out, the species becomes EXTINCT. Increased farming, illegal hunting, and the spread of human settlement has threatened many species with extinction throughout history. In 1965, the International Union for Conservation of Nature established the Red List to monitor plants and animals that might be at risk of extinction and to try to protect them.

GLOSSARY

ABACUS A wooden frame with beads on rods, traditionally used for counting and calculation.

ACCELERATION An increase in speed.

ACHROMATIC LENS An invention designed to bring two different wavelengths of light into common focus.

ACOUSTICS The scientific study of sound, or the way in which a room is suited to the transmission of sound.

ALCHEMY An ancient philosophy based on ideals of purity and perfection. It included magical spells, but also some useful experiments that helped the development of modern chemistry.

ALGEBRA The branch of mathematics in which letters and symbols are used to show relations in equations or formulae.

ALTERNATING CURRENT (AC) A flow of electricity that switches back and forth about 50 times per second.

AMPLITUDE The measurement of changes in air pressure brought about by sound waves.

ANESTHESIA An insensitivity to pain and feeling, brought about by certain drugs, often during an operation.

ANALYTICAL ENGINE A mechanical computer (1837) designed by Charles Babbage.

ANATOMY The science which deals with the structure of any life-form.

ANTIBIOTIC A medication that attacks or kills bacteria.

ANTIKYTHERA MECHANISM A small device made in Greece in the 2nd century BC. It used gears to calculate astronomical positions. It is the earliest known analog computer.

ANTIQUARK An antiparticle which pairs with a quark, to make a particle called a meson.

APEX PREDATOR An animal at the top end of a food chain.

APOTHECARY An old-fashioned word for someone who prepares and dispenses medicines.

ARITHMETIC The branch of mathematics that concerns numbers and sums.

ARITHMOMETER The first mechanical calculator to use a digital system (1820).

ASTROLOGY The study of the stars and planets in the belief that their positions affect humans and events on Earth.

ATOM The smallest unit of an element. It is made up of a nucleus at its core, and particles called neutrons, protons, and electrons.

ATOMIC MODEL The supposed structure of an atom, repeatedly rearranged by physicists over the ages.

AXLE The rod or shaft joining two wheels.

BACTERIUM A microorganism. Some bacteria are harmless and some are good for you, but others bring disease.

BAKELITE (or Baekelite) Invented in 1907, this was an early form of plastic with many everyday uses.

BIG BANG This theory proposes that the universe began with a massive explosion of energy, which is why it is still expanding today.

BINARY CODE A text or computer instruction made up of sequences of two digits: 0 and 1.

BIOMASS Organic material such as wood or plant matter, often used as a fuel in power stations.

BLOOD TRANSFUSION Taking blood from one person and giving it to someone else.

BOMBE An electro-mechanical code-breaking machine developed for World War II by Alan Turing and Gordon Welchman.

BOSON A class of subatomic particles.

BRONZE AGE Any period of history during which the leading technology was the making of bronze—a mixture of copper and tin.

CALCULATOR A small keypad device used to work out sums. Electronic calculators were developed in the 1960s and 1970s.

CALENDAR A table or chart showing days, weeks, months, or years.

CAMERA A device that captures an image and records it on photographic film or with digital signals.

CARBON DIOXIDE A gas (CO_2) made up of one carbon and two oxygen atoms.

CARBON NANOTUBE An extremely strong and tiny cylindrical carbon structure, used in electronics and optics.

CASSETTE A small enclosed tape for audio recording or playing, popular from the 1970s to about 2000.

CD A compact disc. It is a digital optical disc made of plastic, for recorded sound or stored data.

CELL The smallest unit of a plant or animal, enclosed by a membrane or cell wall.

CELL THEORY A theory that the cell is the basic unit of structure and function in all forms of life, and that cells divide to create new ones.

CELL WALL A rigid barrier surrounding the cells of plants, fungi, and bacteria.

CHEMICAL ENERGY Stored energy that is released during a chemical reaction.

CHLOROPLAST One of the tiny parts inside a plant cell that carry out photosynthesis, converting solar energy into glucose.

CHROMATOGRAPHY Separating out colored components of a mixture such as an ink or dye, by passing them through a medium in which they move at different speeds.

CIRCULATORY Passing around a system, as blood when it moves around the body.

COLOR SPECTRUM The part of the electro-magnetic spectrum that includes visible light. Isaac Newton described the colors as red, orange, yellow, green, blue, indigo, and violet.

COMBUSTION A chemical process where a fuel reacts with oxygen to give off heat and light.

COMPOUND A chemical combination of separate elements.

COMPUTER A machine that can be programmed to follow sets of instructions. Electronic computers were developed from the 1940s onward.

COMPUTING Using a computer to calculate or process data by using algorithms (step-by-step operations).

CONCAVE Having a surface that curves inward. Ones which curve outward are called **CONVEX**.

CONDUCTOR A material which can carry the flow of an electric current.

CORNEA The transparent layer at the front of the eye.

COUNTING RODS A series of small bars used for doing sums in ancient China.

CYLINDER PHONOGRAPH The first method of recording and playing back sound, popular until about 100 years ago.

CYTOPLASM The material surrounding the nucleus of a living cell.

DECIBEL A unit of measurement (dB) for the loudness of sound.

DECELERATION A decrease in speed.

DECIMAL SYSTEM The system of numerals based on the number ten.

DIRECT CURRENT (DC) A flow of electricity in one direction.

DISC PHONOGRAPH This soon replaced the cylinder phonograph, and disc records remained popular for most of the 20th century.

DISTILLATION The purification of a liquid by a process of evaporation and condensation.

DNA A molecule of deoxyribonucleic acid—the chemical that carries the genetic programming of all living things.

DOSAGE The amount of medicine to be given to someone.

ECHO A reflected sound that is heard shortly after the original sound.

ECHOLOCATION Using reflected sound waves to map any obstacles ahead. This is used in the natural world by bats and by humans in sonar devices.

ECOLOGY The branch of science that deals with the relationship of organisms to each other and to the environment.

ECOSYSTEM The community and networks of living organisms within an environment.

ELECTRIC DISCHARGE The release and transmission of electricity through gas or another medium.

ELECTRICAL CURRENT The flow of an electrical charge, as carried by electrons along a wire.

ELECTRICAL ENERGY A type of kinetic energy created by the movement of electrical charges.

ELECTROMAGNETISM Electromagnetic forces and the study of them.

ELECTROMAGNETIC SPECTRUM The full range of radiation, which includes gamma rays, X-rays, ultraviolet, Infrared, visible light, microwaves, and radio waves.

ELECTRON A subatomic particle with a negative electric charge.

ELEMENT Any substance that cannot be broken down into simpler substances. Each element is defined by the number of protons in the nucleus of one of its atoms.

THE ENLIGHTENMENT A European movement of the late 17th and 18th centuries, which encouraged science, experimentation, and rational thought.

EMISSION THEORY An early theory which proposed that the eye gives out beams of light in order to see objects.

ENGINE A machine which can transform one form of energy, such as heat, into mechanical energy.

EVAPORATION When a liquid turns into vapor (a gas).

EVOLUTION The way in which life on Earth develops and changes as it adapts to the environment.

EXCRETION The passing of waste matter from the body.

EXPLOSIVE Any substance that can explode, as in a bomb or a firework.

EXTINCT A species, or other group of animals or plants, having died out.

FIBER-OPTIC CABLE A cable carrying one or many optical fibers, used for carrying light.

FILTRATION Using a filter to separate out particles from a liquid or a gas.

FOOD CHAIN The way in which each living thing passes on its energy to other living things as it feeds. Grass may feed a rabbit, which is eaten by a fox.

FORCE Any interaction that makes an object move or change its speed.

FOSSIL Remains or impressions of ancient plants or animals found in rocks and stones.

FOSSIL FUELS Fuels such as **OIL**, **GAS**, or **COAL**, formed millions of years ago from the remains of plants and small creatures.

FREQUENCY The vibration of a sound, measured in hertz (Hz).

FRICTION The force that resists the relative motion of two surfaces when they slide against each other.

FUNGUS One of a range of organisms that vary from tiny yeasts and molds to mushrooms and toadstools.

GAMMA RAY Electromagnetic radiation caused by the radioactive decay of atomic nuclei.

GEAR A mechanism such as a toothed wheel, designed for transmitting or changing motion.

GENE Made of DNA, genes pass on characteristics from one generation to the next.

GENERATOR Any machine used to convert mechanical energy into electrical energy.

GENETICS The study of genes.

GENOME The complete genetic material of an organism.

GEOMETRY The branch of mathematics that deals with shape, size, areas, and volumes.

GEOTHERMAL ENERGY Heat from deep below the Earth's surface, which can provide steam to drive turbines in power stations.

GERM A tiny organism that causes disease.

GLASS-BLOWING Shaping molten glass by blowing air through a pipe.

GLOBAL WARMING The warming of the Earth's surface temperature, by natural or by human causes.

GRAVITATIONAL ENERGY The potential energy of a highly placed object.

GREENHOUSE GAS Any gas that absorbs infrared radiation from the sun and radiates heat, contributing to the problem of global warming. Examples include carbon dioxide and chlorofluorocarbons.

GUNPOWDER An explosive mixture made of charcoal, sulphur, and saltpetre (potassium nitrate, KNO_3).

HERBIVORE Any animal that eats plants.

HEREDITY The passing on of characteristics from one generation to the next.

HERTZ The measurement of audio frequency (Hz), named after Heinrich Hertz (1857–94), who proved the existence of electromagnetic radiation.

HIEROGLYPHIC NUMBERS Numerals written in a system of picture symbols, as used in ancient Egypt.

HUMAN GENOME PROJECT An international research program that aims to map all the genes of the human genome.

HYDROGEN An element (H) that is the most plentiful chemical substance in the universe.

HYDROPOWER ELECTRICITY Generated by turbines, which are powered by the flow of water.

INDUSTRIAL REVOLUTION The age of new factories, mining, and technologies that changed Europe and North America in the 18th and 19th centuries.

INFRARED The part of the electromagnetic spectrum that comes between visible red and microwaves.

INTEGRATED CIRCUIT An electronic circuit made on a small piece of semiconducting material, such as silicon.

INVERTEBRATE Any creatures without a backbone.

IRON AGE Any period of history during which the leading technology was the smelting and working of iron.

KEVLAR™ A tough synthetic fiber used in making tires and clothing.

KEYHOLE SURGERY Carrying out an operation using very small incisions and fiber-optic equipment.

KINETIC ENERGY The energy an object possesses when it is in moving.

LANDFILL SITE A garbage dump where the waste is buried underground.

LATITUDE The distance from the Equator of any position on the Earth's surface. Measured in "degrees" and "minutes."

LAW OF UNIVERSAL GRAVITATION Isaac Newton's attempt in 1687 to explain how the force of gravity works, with each particle attracting every other in proportion to its mass. The law was not revised until 1915.

LAWS OF MOTION Isaac Newton's three physical laws (1687) describe the interaction between an object and the forces acting upon it, and the motion that results.

LENS A curved piece of glass or other transparent material that focuses or disperses a beam of light.

LEPTONS Subatomic particles without strong interactions. Some are like electrons and others are neutral, called neutrinos.

LIGHT-YEAR The distance that light can travel in one year, used as an astronomical measurement.

LONGITUDE The distance from the meridian of any position on the Earth's surface. Measured in "degrees" and "minutes."

MASS A measure of an object's resistance to acceleration when force is applied.

MATERIALS SCIENCE The study of the physics and chemistry of matter, and its use in engineering and industry.

MECHANICAL ENERGY The combination of kinetic energy and potential energy in any object which is used to do work.

MEDIUM A substance through which something such as light or sound is transmitted.

MEMBRANE A thin layer of tissue that lines or partitions parts of an organism.

METAL A mineral that is often hard, shiny, and able to conduct electricity.

MICROCHIP A small piece of silicon or other material which contains an integrated circuit for use in a computer.

MICROORGANISM A microscopic life-form such as a bacterium or virus.

MICROSCOPE An instrument that is used to study very small objects.

MICROWAVES Part of the electromagnetic spectrum, used for cooking, radar, and navigation.

MILKY WAY Our home galaxy, made up of between 100 billion and 400 billion stars.

MITOCHONDRIA Tiny rods inside a living cell which are responsible for generating energy.

MIXTURE A combination of substances that are not combined chemically.

MORSE CODE A code in which letters are represented by long or short signals using flashes of light or sound pulses. Originally developed for the telegraph, it became wisely used in radio communications.

MOLECULE The smallest particle in an element or a compound that has the chemical properties of that substance. It is made up of atoms that are bonded together.

MOVING PICTURES ("Movies") An early name for cinema. The film was a series of still images that, when projected onto a screen, looked as if they were moving.

MULTIPLE PULLEY CRANE Cranes that use an assembly of pulleys to raise heavy loads.

MUTATION A change in the structure of a gene, which may be inherited.

MYLAR™ A kind of stretched polyester film or plastic sheeting.

NANOMACHINE A machine sized between one-thousandth and one-millionth of a millimeter.

NANOTECHNOLOGY Technology that works on a tiny scale, at the level of atoms and molecules

NAPIER'S BONES A mechanical calculator invented in 1617 and used for multiplication and division.

NATURAL SELECTION The way in which life-forms which are well adapted to their environment tend to survive and succeed.

NEGATIVE NUMBER Any number that is less than zero, written with a minus symbol.

NEUTRON A subatomic particle with no electrical charge.

NUCLEAR AGE The period of history beginning in 1945, when the USA dropped two atomic bombs on Japan, and the start of civil nuclear power in the 1950s.

NUCLEAR FISSION The breaking up of an atomic nucleus into small parts, as the result of radioactive decay or a nuclear reaction.

NUCLEAR FUSION The bringing together of two or more atoms so that new nuclei and particles are formed, releasing energy.

NUCLEAR POWER The use of nuclear reactors to generate the heat needed to operate steam turbines, generating electricity.

NUCLEUS (1) The central core of an atom, containing protons and neutrons, and orbited by electrons. (2) The central core of a cell in a living organism.

NUTRITION Obtaining the goodness in foods (nutrients) that helps all living things to function and survive.

NYLON A type of synthetic polymer used to make fiber, molded shapes, or film for packaging.

OMO REMAINS Fossil remains found near the Omo River in Ethiopia. They include the oldest known remains of *Homo sapiens*, which are about 195,000 years old.

OPTIC NERVE The nerve that carries information from the retina to the brain.

ORE Any rock that contains a metal, such as iron.

ORGAN Any part of a plant or animal which has a specific function, such as a heart or a lung.

ORGANISM Any form of life and the parts that keep it alive.

OXYGEN An element (O) making up over 20 percent of the Earth's atmosphere.

OZONE LAYER Part of the Earth's atmosphere that absorbs the most ultraviolet radiation from the sun. It has a relatively high level of a gas called ozone (O_3).

PAINKILLER A medicine that relieves pain.

PALAEOLITHIC ERA The Old Stone Age, a period in which the leading technology (for humans and pre-humans) was crude stone tools. It is currently assessed as lasting from about 3.3 million to about 10,000 years ago.

PARTICLE A general term for any very small piece of matter. The word often refers to atoms or to even smaller (subatomic) particles, such as electrons.

PERIODIC TABLE A chart showing the elements grouped according to their atomic numbers (numbers of protons).

PHOTON A particle that is the basis of all electromagnetic radiation, including light.

PITCH The measure of a sound's frequency, making it seem either high or low.

PLACE VALUE A numerical system in which the value of a number is shown by its position in relation to a point.

PLASTICS A wide range of materials, mostly synthetic and derived from petrochemicals.

POLYMER A large molecule made up of many repeated links. Polymers occur naturally, but also in synthetic plastics

POSITIVE NUMBER Any number greater than zero.

POTENTIAL ENERGY Energy possessed by an object in its current position rather than in motion.

POTTER'S WHEEL A revolving disc on which pottery can be shaped in the round.

POWER STATION An industrial plant used for generating electricity.

PRISM An angled piece of glass or other transparent material that refracts light, breaking it up into a spectrum of colors.

PROPERTIES OF MATERIALS The physical characteristics of materials, such as elasticity or stiffness.

PROTON A subatomic particle that has a positive electrical charge.

PULLEY SYSTEM An arrangement of grooved wheels designed to change the direction of a rope when hauled. It is used to raise heavy loads.

PUSHING FORCE A force applied to an object to move it forward, away from the pusher.

QUANTUM PHYSICS The mechanics of atoms and subatomic particles.

QUARK A subatomic particle of matter that combines with others to form composite particles called hadrons.

RADIATION The giving out of energy as waves or particles.

RADIANT ENERGY Energy as given out in electromagnetic waves.

RADIO In a radio broadcast, electromagnetic radio waves are altered to make up a signal. When this is picked up by an antenna, it can be converted back it to its original form.

RADIOACTIVE Giving out dangerous radiation, as happens when an unstable atomic nucleus decays, or as the result of a nuclear reaction.

RADIO WAVES Part of the electromagnetic spectrum, used for communications and broadcasting.

RECORD A disc used in a phonograph. A needle picks up sound vibrations from the grooves of the disc, which are amplified. Discs made of shellac were replaced by vinyl in the 1950s, which has become popular again today.

RECYCLE The conversion of waste products into materials or objects that can be used again.

REFLECTION When light waves strike a surface such as a mirror and bounce back into the medium from which they came.

REFLECTOR TELESCOPE A telescope that uses a mirror to collect and focus light.

REFRACTION The bending of a light wave when it passes through another medium, such as water or glass.

RENEWABLE ENERGY Energy that does not rely on finite fuels such as coal or oil, but on ongoing sources such as sunlight, tides, or wind.

REPRODUCTION Producing offspring, either sexually or asexually.

RESPIRATION A process of producing energy in living organisms. Humans breathe in oxygen and breathe out carbon dioxide.

RETINA The light-sensitive tissue that lines the eye.

SEXTANT An instrument used for navigation. It can measure the angle between the horizon and the sun, moon, planets, or stars.

SILICON (SI) An element classed as a metalloid—a substance which is metal-like. It is used in making integrated circuits for computers and mobile phones.

SIMPLE MACHINE Any basic mechanical device used to increase force, such as lever or a wedge.

SLIDE RULE A ruler with a sliding strip in the middle, used to multiply, divide, and carry out complicated calculations at speed.

SMELT To separate metal from its ore by heating.

SOLAR ENERGY Heat or light from the sun, which can be captured to provide a renewable source of electricity or heat.

SOLAR SYSTEM The sun and everything that orbits around it, such as planets, moons, and asteroids.

SONAR (SOund Navigation And Ranging) The use of reflected sound waves to detect objects underwater.

SONIC BOOM The loud noise created by a sound wave after an aircraft flies faster than the speed of sound.

SOUND BARRIER The increased drag which affects aircraft as they approach the speed of sound.

SOUND ENERGY Energy created by a sound wave.

SPOKED WHEEL An open wheel in which the hub is linked to the rim by bars or rods.

STATIC ELECTRICITY A stationary or atmospheric electrical charge.

STEAM LOCOMOTIVE A railway engine that uses steam power from its boiler to haul its load.

SUBATOMIC PARTICLE Particles that are smaller than an atom, such as electrons or photons.

SUBSTANCE What something is made of—matter or material.

SYSTEM A combination of parts that together perform a function.

TAXONOMY The scientific classification of living things.

TEFLON™ Invented in 1938, this synthetic compound of chlorine and fluorine makes a nonstick coating for pots and pans.

TELEPHONE A long-distance communications device that converts the spoken word into electronic signals and convert them back again at the other end. Landline phones were invented in the 19th century and mobile phones in the 1970s.

TELESCOPE An instrument used for viewing distant objects, using lenses and sometimes mirrors.

THEORY OF RELATIVITY Revolutionary ideas proposed by Albert Einstein (1879–1955) about space, time, gravity, energy, and mass.

THERMAL ENERGY The energy that comes from heat.

THERMOMETER Any instrument that measures temperature.

THERMOSCOPE An instrument that shows a change in temperature, often through the use of a liquid in a tube.

TISSUE The organic materials that make up any life-form.

TRANSFORMER A device used to vary alternating voltage for electric power.

TREE OF LIFE Describes the relationships between both living and extinct organisms through the metaphor of a tree. As described in Charles Darwin's book *On the Origin of Species* (1859).

TURBINE A wheel or rotor fitted with vanes, made to spin around by a flow of water or gases. Turbines may be used to generate electricity.

ULTRASOUND IMAGING A way for doctors to view inside the body, using images from high-frequency sound waves.

ULTRAVIOLET The part of the electromagnetic spectrum which comes between visible light and X-rays.

VACCINE A preparation that makes one immune from a disease.

VERTEBRATE Any creatures with a backbone.

VIBRATION A periodic shaking movement, as in an earth tremor or a sound wave.

VIRUS A microorganism that occupies living cells and infects them.

VOLT (V) The unit of measurement for electric potential or electromotive force.

VOLTAIC PILE Probably the first type of electric chemical battery, invented by Alessandro Volta in 1800.

WATER MILL A mill that uses a water wheel to drive a mechanical process, such as grinding grain into flour.

WATER WHEEL A wheel turned by flowing water, used to power machinery or raise buckets of water.

WAVES Electromagnetic radiation travels in waves. The distance from a point on one wave to the same point on the next wave is called a wavelength.

WIND TURBINE A turbine that uses the kinetic energy of wind to generate electricity.

X-RAYS Part of the electromagnetic spectrum, used for medical examination of bones and tissues.

ZERO A symbol representing nought (0). No quantity.

With thanks to John Gillespie —L.J.G.

Quarto is the authority on a wide range of topics.
Quarto educates, entertains and enriches the lives of
our readers—enthusiasts and lovers of hands-on living.
www.quartoknows.com

First published in the United States in 2017 by Wide Eyed Editions
an imprint of Quarto Inc., 142 W 36th St, 4th Floor, New York, NY 10018, USA
QuartoKnows.com • Visit our blogs at QuartoKnows.com

ISBN 978-1-84780-843-1

The illustrations were created with mixed media
Set in Lunchbox

Designed by Nicola Price
Edited by Jenny Broom
Published by Rachel Williams

Printed in China

1 3 5 7 9 8 6 4 2